savannah syncopators

AFRICAN RETENTIONS IN THE BLUES

PAUL OLIVER

𝔰𝔡

STEIN AND DAY / *Publishers* / New York

First published, in both hard cover and paperback editions, in the United States of America by Stein and Day / *Publishers* / 1970.

Printed in England
Stein and Day / *Publishers* / 7 East 48 Street, New York, N.Y. 10017
SBN 8128-1315-4 (hard cover)
     8128-1319-7 (paperback)

Produced by November Books Limited
Designed by Ian Cameron
House editor: Elizabeth Kingsley-Rowe

Photographs
By the author: 4, 8, 13, 26, 30, 33, 34, 44, 53, 54, 65, 66 (left), 78, 80, 82, 85, 87, 92, 99, 101
From the author's collection: 7, 18, 22, 23
Library of Congress: 24
Disques Ocora: 50, 51, 59, 62, 94; (photographer Tolia Nikiprowetzky) 29, 66 (right) (photographer Charles Duvelle)
William Russell: 38
Maps drawn by the Author: 40, 43, 69
Chris Strachwitz (Arhoolie Records): 79, 83, 95, 97, 100

CONTENTS

AFTERNOON - NANGODI

Kunaal was a Fra-Fra, a member of a tiny sub-tribe in the Awuna complex of Grunshi tribes – though only the long scar that ran from the side of his nose to his jawline indicated it to those who could recognise the scarifications. His long features and high, broad cheekbones, the long upper lip and the shrewd eyes, emphasised his savannah heritage, though his clothes were adapted European. An ill-fitting grey suit jacket, which he had marked out in large tacking stitches, a pair of khaki shorts and a hat completed the outfit. Made of translucent green plastic, the mock trilby hat allowed no ventilation and the perspiration streamed down his face from under the brim, as he threw from one hand to the other at great speed a calabash rattle filled with beans. By agitating the rattle between fingers, palms and the fleshier parts of the hand, he produced a succession of rapid and extraordinarily loud rhythms. His companion, Sosira, also bore the Grunshi scar on his face for he, too, was a Fra-Fra. Sosira wore the loose, coarsely woven smock made up from bands of indigo and white striped cotton cloth that was fairly common among the men of the region. His head was bound in a close turban and he looked cooler

The Fra-Fra musicians, Kunaal (left) and Sosira. Nangodi Ghana, 1964.

4

and more comfortable than Kunaal. More serious, too, for it was evident that Kunaal wore his modified European clothes with humour, conscious of the curious figure that he cut. Both men sang, but the burden of the singing was carried by Sosira whose slightly hoarse high phrases were placed against those of the two-stringed fiddle that he played at waist level. Fashioned from a small gourd over which a skin membrane had been tightly drawn, and with an arm to which the strings were held in tension by hide tuning rings, the fiddle was decorated with strips of coloured cloth, fragments of skins and a cow's tail. With a small semi-circular bow of animal hair, Sosira played an accompaniment of repeated melodic-rhythmic phrases, stopping the strings with fingers that slid momentarily along them to produce subtly wailing, whining notes.

A crowd of men gathered to listen from the neighbouring compounds of cylindrical mud houses sculptured on the dusty laterite land. They sat beneath a shady tree, some nearly naked, some in shirts and trousers imported to the market from the coast four hundred miles to the south. For the village of Nangodi where Kunaal and Sosira were playing that day in May 1964 was in the extreme north of Ghana, just five miles from the border with Upper Volta, deep in the savannah parkland belt which gives way to the desert, another couple of hundred miles to the north. I was there with a specific purpose: to gain information on the problems of communication with the Grunshi tribes, whose minimal economy and agriculture at bare subsistence level in the hot, arid zone was to be the subject of a resettlement programme. Eventually I was to instruct African architectural and planning students from the southern Akan tribes in techniques which might establish basic communication systems. But I was also engaged in recording the music of the peoples with whom I was working and in conducting lines of research which had arisen from my studies in Afro-American music. For me the hours in which the unflagging Kunaal and Sosira played that afternoon as we passed around calabashes of millet beer were immensely exciting. It wasn't only the heady brew which made my brain sing in the heat of the overhead sun; it was also the thrill of making what was for me a discovery which gave the first inkling of an answer to a fundamental problem that I had encountered a while before.

Although I was a visiting lecturer in the Faculty of Architecture at the University of Science and Technology in Kumasi, the capital of the Ashanti region, I had also spent a month as a visiting lecturer in the Department of African Studies at the University of Ghana in Legon near Accra, a hundred-odd miles to the south, close to the coast. There I had given daily lectures in Afro-American music, with particular emphasis on the blues, American Negro folk song, gospel music and early jazz, and held regular seminars with a group of students who were engaged in studies of Ghanaian music. The opportunity to do some field work in this area of study had been an exciting one and the facilities at Legon were exceptional. Under the guidance of Professor Kwabena Nketia, the most erudite African writer and student of African music, the work being undertaken was varied and serious. Visiting musicians from many parts of the country stayed on the campus and demonstrated their music which was thus available for the analysis of the students. Ga, Ewe, Ashanti, Fanti, Nzima and other Akan tribes were accessible and their many musical traditions were still much alive within miles of the coast.

The seminars with the students of the Department, almost all of whom came from the Akan tribes, and particularly from Ashanti, proved to be very perplexing. Accustomed as they were to the music of their own peoples but trained, too, in Western techniques of recording and analysis, they were in an ideal position both to detect and to identify 'African' retentions in jazz. But seldom was there more than a ripple of positive response, and even when there was it was generally conceded that the differences vastly outweighed any points of similarity. By examining some West Indian musical forms where the retentions were clear and identifiable and relating these to examples of New Orleans jazz by veteran musicians, it was possible to agree on generalities concerning the rhythmic use of front line instruments, or the polyrhythmic texture of piano, guitar, bass and drums. Eventually some of the generalisations made concerning the relationships of African music to jazz could be substantiated in outline, but the positive evidence that I had sought and hoped for was elusive

If this applied to jazz, it applied with even greater disparity to the blues. Interested as I had been in African arts, building and music for many years, I had long been puzzled by the gulf between African music, as represented by the drum orchestras, and the blues. African work songs seemed to supply some tangible link with the American Negro vocal traditions, and in the hand-clapping 'praise shouting' of congregations in Negro churches echoes of Africa could be heard. By extension from these one could trace uncertainly some tenuous threads which linked

6

African vocal approaches with the blues, but I could not share the confidence of those who could detect pure Africanisms in the singing of Blind Willie Johnson or Charley Patton. Still more perplexing was the music that could be heard in the villages of the rain forest and coastal belts in Ghana and the neighbouring territories of Ivory Coast and Dahomey, and to the east, Nigeria. Drum orchestras with *atumpan* 'talking' drums and tunable tension drums produced no comparable sounds with the instrumental techniques and traditions of the blues singers, the songsters, the ragtime banjoists and guitarists, or, as far as one could determine, their antecedents.

Yet along the coast could be seen the great stone castles of Christiansborg, Anomabu, Elmina, Dixcove and many others; storybook castles bristling with ancient black cannon between the castellations of their white walls and keeps, still trained on the beaches and the approaches. Charming monuments now; but down low near the water-level can still be seen the dank, evil-smelling dungeons where slaves were herded to await shipment to the Americas on the Middle Passage. And running through the massive walls, dripping and slime-covered, remain the tunnels that led straight to the holds of the ships, down which the slaves took their last steps in Africa. This was the Guinea Coast, the Slave Coast that stretched by way of Whydah and the lagoons of Lagos round the bend of Africa, south to the Gabon. This was the land from which the slaves were shipped; if there were any surviving links with the blues, surely they should be here? This was the problem and it was not until I made the trip to Bolgatanga, Navrongo and Nangodi that a possible line of enquiry that might eventually lead to a solution presented itself. Later, after a while in the Yoruba country of eastern Nigeria, I travelled to Kano, the great Hausa city in the northern region of Nigeria from which the camel trains set off to cross the Sahara. Here, too, I found

'The South-west Prospect of James Ifland on the River of Gambia, 1727'.

Photo: Elimina Castle, Ghana. Slaves were kept in the dungeons (left) and herded into the walled compound (right) before shipment.

further support for a new approach to the question of African retentions in the blues.

Both before and since my stay in West Africa, I have been engaged in a project with the Houston folklorist, Mack McCormick. This was, and is, a detailed study of the blues and related Negro secular music in Texas and adjacent territories. Thorough research in a vast and little-studied area – as far as blues is concerned – has involved us in a far more lengthy and complex work than we had anticipated. During the course of it, many problems presented themselves, some common to blues history as a whole, some peculiar to Texas. Texas was settled late in the history of the South, and much of its population did not arrive until the Civil War. On the other hand, a small but not insignificant body of planters and slave-owners had been in the bottomlands of the Texas rivers for many years before. The question arose of how many of the slaves that they held, and that were in Texas at the time of Emancipation, had come directly from Africa; or were they the sons and daughters of slaves whose memories of Africa still survived ? What retentions were there of African traditions in the blues in Texas ? It was in anticipation of finding some answer to these questions from the African end that I journeyed so eagerly to Ghana. However, the drum orchestras, the music of the funerals, the festivals and the 'fetish' dances in Ashanti only added to the confusion which a study of the writings of jazz historians had already created.

I cannot claim to have solved the problems surrounding the question of African retentions in the blues. Only after detailed research in both the United States and in West Africa might a positive conclusion be reached. This monograph does no more than attempt to lay out some aspects of the questions arising for re-examination, and perhaps serve as a guide to future research. Basically, it may be summarised as a prelude to a study of African retentions in jazz and the blues, for it attempts to raise the fundamental questions: What is meant by 'Africa'? Where in Africa can musical forms related to the blues be found? Is there any justification for assuming that slaves came from these regions, if they exist? Can African peoples be considered as homogeneous, or do they divide into specific groups? Can African music be considered as homogeneous, or does its character vary over the territories which supplied the slaves? Are there any character-istics of music and instrumentation that do, or do not, accord with those in North America? If musical forms related to the blues can be found, is there any basis for the assumption that slaves came from these regions? Were there circumstances in North America that would inhibit African retentions and were there any that would promote them?

In general this book looks in outline and approximately in this order at these questions. But much has been written already by anthropologists, ethnomusicologists and jazz historians on African retentions in North American music, especially jazz, and it is necessary therefore to look at some of these writings and the questions that they, too, raise. And all this discussion is based on the assumption that retentions of African culture, or a part of it, do exist and can be established. But if they are proven, by what means were they transmitted? This, perhaps, is the first question that should be examined. If there seemed to be, in the music of Kunaal and Sosira, some fragile link with the music of the blues, was it by accident, was it coincidence, was it a direct ancestral tradition shared in Africa and by the slaves in America, or was it an innate capacity for producing music of a particular kind? It was the question that presented itself then, and it was one to which there is as yet no definitive answer. But the following is a sketch of the lines of research that might be pursued, and which, given the opportunity, I hope one day to undertake.

AFRICA AND THE JAZZ HISTORIAN

In a monument to racial prejudice, Madison Grant stated in 1916 that 'whether we like to admit it or not, the result of the mixture of two races, in the long run, gives us a race reverting to the more ancient, generalized and lower type. The cross between a white man and an Indian is an Indian; the cross between a white man and a Negro is a Negro.' *The Passing of the Great Race* summed up unequivocally the American attitude to the identity of the black man. Within the world of blues and blues singers there are those who sing and those who listen who represent every shade from black to near white, whose designation, legally or by custom, is Negro. Notwithstanding the illogicality and the lack of any scientific basis in the belief, a man is a Negro if he has any perceptible or known Negro blood in him. Yet pure-blood Negro stock in the United States is exceptionally rare today and some white ancestry is known in the family tree of a large proportion of Negro families. When the anthropologist Melville Herskovits prepared his *Anthropometry of the American Negro*, he concluded that over seventy percent of his informants had knowledge of white persons in their ancestry. This and other evidence was sifted by the team led by Gunnar Myrdal who substantially agreed with his findings and with the general conclusion that the majority of 'Negroes' so designated have perhaps one-third white blood, while some have considerably more and others much less.

It is popularly assumed that the Negro has an innate sense of rhythm; that his capacity for music and dance, for athletic performance and even sexual performance relates to inherent abilities. Whether these are diminished or diluted by the presence of more or less white blood is seldom questioned in the folk myth, for the Negro is a Negro and the question does not arise. The belief that cultural traits can be inherited is generally discounted by the anthropologist. Though he was dedicated to Negro studies, Herskovits questioned von Hornbostel's earlier propositions on this point. 'It has been claimed by Professor von Hornbostel that the spirituals of the United States are essentially European folk-songs created by the innate musical genius of the African, and that only the motor behaviour which biologically determines the manner in which they are sung is African. But would this type of motor behaviour persist in crossing? For the appearance of the mixed Negroes and the pure ones when singing these songs is quite the same,' he commented, posing the fundamental question, 'what is innate and what is cultural?'.

If the present studies which pursue the nature of biological rhythms in animals are extended to mankind's creative capacities, it is feasible that one day the evidence may again substantiate the belief that rhythm may be transmitted culturally. Even if this does turn out to be the case, Herskovits' question as to whether it would survive transmission through ethnic dilution still stands. At present such a view is not favoured by anthropologists, who would generally support the argument that cultural traits are learned rather than inherent. The process of enculturation through which the habits of one generation, its values and its customs, are passed on to subsequent ones may account for the persistence of some cultural elements, while the process of acculturation, whereby the meeting of cultures may lead to the evolution of a new one, is also accepted. To these may be added the process of cultural diffusion, or the spread of culture by imitation and influence. These together may indicate the manner in which Negro cultural patterns have taken the forms that they have in the United States. In the persistence of mannerisms of song, or musical technique; in the continuance of traditional modes of expression and vehicles of creativity – as for instance, the church songs or the work songs – enculturation is seen at work. As the African's music met that of his American masters; as his language became modified and adapted to a new language to persist in some ways of phrasing in a culturally distinct argot; or in the way in which the ballads have assumed the western structure and the blues have been constructed upon the European tetrachord, the process of acculturation is witnessed. And as the blues spread, or the gospel songs moved from city churches to country congregations, just as the earlier shouting services had been transmitted from the rural to the urban places of worship; as jazz moved up-river or fanned out across the southern and the northern states, the principle of diffusion is repeatedly demonstrated.

In a sense, this might suffice as evidence of process. But it does not explain what is transmitted, welded or diffused, nor does it explain where the origins of the elements that have been so passed on actually lie. If certain of these characteristics in Negro music, and in the blues of the present century, are above all characteristic of the 'Negro', it is appropriate to question where and how they arose. Few jazz historians, at any rate, have been in doubt that 'Africa' is the source of most of these cultural characteristics which have shaped Negro jazz. In his pioneering *Shining Trumpets*, Rudi Blesh devoted a chapter to African origins, with many other references to African elements throughout his study of traditional jazz. To support his thesis, he drew extensively on the recordings made by the Herskovits in Dahomey in 1931, and on Mieczyslaw Kolinksi's analysis of them. In *The Story of Jazz*, Marshall Stearns devoted three chapters to African origins and survivals, again making extensive use of Herskovits' writings and adding earlier documentary evidence in the writings of George Washington Cable and others, notably the former's much-quoted *The Dance in Place Congo*. More recently, among numerous jazz histories, Gunther Schuller has, in *Early Jazz*, followed this line of argument, but has used as his principle source, the Reverend A. M. Jones' *Studies in African Music* which is based mainly on a group of dances of the Ewe people of eastern Ghana.

As these writers were primarily concerned with the history of jazz, and with its New Orleans origins specifically, the quotations from Cable or Latrobe which described Congo Square, or, as in Robert Goffin's *Jazz – From the Congo to the Metropolitan*, the descriptive writings of Lafcadio Hearn also, are entirely appropriate to the context. These emphasise the drumming that was long a tourist attraction in Congo Square, New Orleans, and the conclusions that may be drawn as to the influence of African derived music on military brass and parade music, when jazz began to emerge as a musical form of distinctive character at the close of the nineteenth century. For their arguments, the studies made by Herskovits in Dahomey or the West Indies, of Harold Courlander in Haiti or Father Jones in Ghana amply supported the contention that the rhythmic character of New Orleans jazz, the multi-lineal structure of its instrumentation and the melodic-rhythmic nature of jazz improvisation were essentially 'African' in origin. These contentions could be borne out and can be explained readily enough in terms of enculturation and acculturation.

When it comes to the blues, the jazz historians are generally shorter on detailed analysis, although the assumption that the blues pre-dated jazz ('the more we learn the earlier it seems to have been', wrote Stearns) has necessitated the ascribing of African origins. 'The blues harmony, like that of its source, the

12

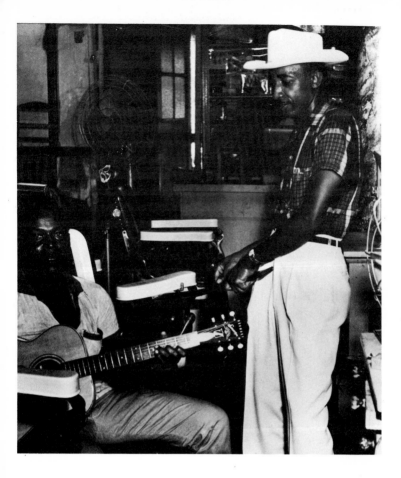

Tractor-driver R. C. Smith played guitar in a Mississippi barber-shop while barber Wade Walton stropped a razor in rhythm. They had not met before, but played in perfect accord – the result of a shared culture or the proverbial 'innate sense of rhythm'?

spiritual, combines with melodies of a pentatonic character. These melodies do not extend beyond the five-note span of the tetrachord and in their formation clearly refer to West African melody', Rudi Blesh stated. Marshall Stearns took a different view: comparing Leadbelly's holler, *Ain't Goin' Down To The Well No More*, he stated that 'identical melodic phrases occur in a 1947 recording by Chano Pozo, who belonged to a Nigerian cult in Havana'. But for Stearns, 'the harmony employed in the blues is another matter.

It is pretty clearly derived from European music although colored by the tonality of the cry. At its simplest the harmony of the blues consists of the three basic chords of our musical language.'

A comparison of observations on the nature of the 'blue note', or flattened seventh, in the blues underlines the confusion and disagreement among writers as to the extent of African influence. Winthrop Sargeant, who argued a 'blues scale' in *Jazz Hot and Hybrid*, studied a number of African recordings to conclude that 'though the blues scale is not indicated anywhere, the preference for one of its components – the flat seventh – is quite marked.' He added that 'among the crude harmonic combinations used one of the most prominent – the dominant seventh, or ninth chord – points strikingly toward certain peculiarities of blues harmonization.' It was not a view shared by André Hodeir. 'Compared with the singers of the Dark Continent, the most authentic of the blues singers would be considered "Europeanized". Don't the blues themselves, with their blue notes, represent quite a deviation from African songs?' he asked, stating confidently 'as we know, these blue notes resulted from the difficulty experienced by the Negro when the hymns taught him by the missionaries made him sing the third and seventh degrees of the scale used in European music, since these degrees do not occur in the primitive five-note scale.' Perhaps the most original proposition of all is Gunther Schuller's, when he considers it 'worth mentioning that Indo-Pakistani music is divided into six principal modes, three of which – afternoon modes – are nothing but the blues scale. To establish a possible historic link between these modes and the American Negro's blues scale might be an interesting project for a future student of jazz.' In view of his dependence on the work of A. M. Jones, it is surprising that he was unaware of the studies made by Jones on the influence of Polynesian and Melanesian music on that of Africa through the employment of the gapped heptatonic scale in the Oceanic and African xylophone.

Gunther Schuller discards as untenable Ernest Borneman's position that 'the only true jazz is Spanish- or Latin-American-influenced jazz,' and states that he is 'on shaky ground when he attempts to develop a theory that, as early as the Middle Ages, African music had a strong influence on Arabic music' and that 'there were all kinds of African strains in the music of Spain which the Negro slaves on arrival in the Caribbean recognised immediately as a sort of musical second cousin.' Developed in his article 'Creole Echoes' and in *Just Jazz 3*, Borneman's theory argued that jazz derived in New Orleans from a Creole source which the African and Spanish acculturation in the West Indies had inspired. In earlier writings Borneman, who had studied with Erich von Hornbostel, had advanced this theory to some extent but had laid greater emphasis in *An Anthropologist Looks at Jazz*, and subsequently, in 'The Roots of Jazz', on the West African influence on jazz. For Borneman 'the complex structure of all traditional twelve-bar blues could hardly have been evolved without the survival of a third Africanism – rhythmic variations on a metric theme.' Borneman gave more attention to African elements in blues than have most writers on jazz, though his references were largely concerned with instrumental blues in jazz. Speaking of the tonic, sub-dominant, dominant sequence of the blues he generalised that in African singing this progression 'will add the diminished seventh to the tonic in his first line, to the sub-dominant in the second and to the dominant in the third. Thus he arrives at the peculiar harmonic structure of the blues.' Neat – but he gave no indication that this experiment had ever been carried out by 'an African'. He did, however, give due attention to the characteristics of African singing and their relationship to blues vocals.

Unfortunately, the connections between African music and the blues have been little researched or considered by anthropologists, especially those with experience in the field in both Africa and the United States. Harold Courlander could have been the exception, but, though he is instructive on the relationship of African work song to Negro work song in the United States in his *Negro Folk Music* of 1963, his chapter on the blues might have been written two decades before, so little does it take into consideration the research undertaken on the subject. So it happens that a paper written by Richard Alan Waterman on 'African Influence on the Music of the Americas' as far back as 1952 has not been superseded. In his paper, Waterman identified a number of characteristics of African music which 'set it off markedly from that of Europe'. These included: dominance of percussion; polymeter; off-beat phrasing of melodic accents; overlapping call and response patterns and above all, what Waterman has termed the 'metronome sense'. These elements could be identified in the music of many countries with Negro populations. In 'Brazil all traits of African music have been retained, and many songs are sung in West African languages. Negro songs of Dutch Guiana exhibit all listed traits of West African music; they are, however, sung in a creolized language, compounded for the most part of English vocabulary

that there are elements in common in the musics of the tribes and peoples who were enslaved to an extent where generalisations can be made about African music. Though the survivals of the customs and rites of particular cults in individual tribes are identified, the survivals in the music are assumed to be universally applicable in Africa, or else in West Africa.

Thirdly, the comments are generally made from the point of view of the anthropologist, or from that of the jazz historian. In the former case, the survivals in the Americas as a whole are generally classified with special reference to the West Indies; in the latter, the viewpoint is conditioned by the need to seek and identify retentions in instrumental jazz, and any reference to them in blues is secondary. Blues, in jazz histories, is usually seen as a precursor of jazz and an influence upon it, rather than as a music with parallel development. It therefore appears as a link between the slavery period and the end of the nineteenth century. In order to fulfil this selected role it must represent certain aspects of the African heritage. Emphasis is placed on the quality of blues singing and the 'vocalised tone' of jazz instrumentation.

It is not the purpose of the present study to attempt to discredit these conclusions or to dispute them. Ample data supporting these contentions have been presented in the works cited as in others.

Kid Ory's Original Creole Jazz Band from New Orleans. The trumpet player, 'Mutt' Carey, used a mute to produce 'vocalised' sounds.

However, the question remains as to whether these 'African' elements persist in the *blues* in the manner they describe. Again, it may be questioned whether the image of the blues as portrayed in these writings is in any way accurate, and whether any survivals from Africa exist in the music which have not been identified in them. If the arguments in support of African retentions are applicable to jazz in New Orleans, they are not necessarily equally applicable to blues. Though from the jazz historian's point of view the relationship between the two musical forms exists, there is nevertheless a great deal of difference between them. Jazz, at least in its early phases, was primarily a group music, using brass and wind instruments with rhythm background, employing improvisational techniques both collectively and in solo. If the histories are correct, solos on clarinet or trumpet were relatively rare in the early phase and the emphasis was on collective improvisation in a polyphonic organisation of a three-part 'front line' against a 'rhythm section'. All instruments tended to play rhythmically, although the role of the front line instruments was to state the theme and improvise upon it. Such jazz bands performed a social function and were used both for street parades and for dances or balls. According to William Russell, the 'brass bands' played for parades and were fully augmented with French horns, trombones and sousaphones, side and snare drums, etc., following a military brass band pattern, while the 'string bands' played for dances and had a trumpet-clarinet-trombone front line, but with the rhythm filled out with guitar or banjo (in some reports with the guitar *preceding* the banjo), string bass and one or two violins.

From this it will be seen that the complex structure of the front line music is not a part of the blues as normally executed, while the brass band music has only the most tenuous links with blues. String bands playing jazz came somewhat closer, in view of their instrumentation; but the blues uses stringed instruments in a melodic-rhythmic manner with a fairly complex finger-picking, whereas the use of guitars and banjos in jazz was almost exclusively used for rhythmic purposes. Much has been made of the vocalised techniques of cornet and trumpet playing and of the use of mutes to achieve crying and choked vocal effects. This has been compared with the use of 'talking drums' in Africa, though these have as their basis pitch and tone elements of language and are not 'vocalised' in the jazz sense. In the use of mutes in jazz, the vocal sounds tend to be imitative and the blues content abstract. In the blues, as a separate music, both the voice and the literal content of the sung lyric are fundamentally important and instruments frequently supply a support to the vocal to extend its content.

It is not to be denied that blues has been a continuing influence on jazz, but it must also be recognised that the influence of jazz on blues has been relatively small. Blues has had an independent life of its own which has met jazz tangentially many times and has provided a source of inspiration, and even fundamental character, to jazz. Nevertheless, the blues has not had an especially important history in New Orleans, but throughout its life has had a far wider distribution. Histories of jazz have always laid emphasis on the origins of the music in New Orleans, but adequate and parallel investigation of jazz in other regions – Florida or the south-west for instance – has not been undertaken. But the case for New Orleans is apparently well established and has had a wealth of documentation in its support. As blues was far more widely distributed, it would seem that either the stimulus of blues on instrumental music was less appreciated elsewhere in the early years of jazz, or that the course of the two musical forms was really very different: the one localised and concentrated, the other diffuse and growing steadily in many parts of the South. So it seems that we are considering not one tradition which had blues preceding and leading to jazz, but two fairly distinct but contiguous traditions. Jazz had origins rooted in parade music, ragtime and dance music, and blues had origins rooted vocally in work songs, and instrumentally in stringed traditions: fiddle, banjo and guitar in particular.

Henry A. Kmen, in his exceptionally well documented *Music in New Orleans*, clearly demonstrated that the stringed traditions existed even in New Orleans in the early decades of the history of the city's slaves. 'As early as 1799 fifes and fiddles were used', he reported, 'and in time banjos, triangles, jews harps and tambourines were added. Moreover observers tell of seeing jigs, fandangoes, and Virginia breakdowns in the square', though from the tunes they played he concluded that 'however much of the primitive there was in the Congo Square dances, it seems apparent that they were borrowing rapidly from the culture around them'. Examples given of Negro dances make frequent mention of violins and banjos, and one of the first of the New Orleans balls described as early as 1802 had an orchestra of six Negro musicians mainly playing fiddles. We read of slaves supplying an orchestra of violins, a flute, triangle and tambourine for a plantation party just

20

outside the city; or fiddle, fife, and flute for a New Year's serenade; or 'Virginia breakdown music' for one of their own Christmas parties. It is not surprising, then, to find references to musical ability in the advertisements of slaves who had escaped or who were up for sale. A random dozen of these notices from 1810–20 show that most played violin, but the tambourine, fife, and drums are also mentioned. To read of a slave escaping with only his clothing and a violin, or attempting to carry with him both a violin and tambourine reveals much. Gabriel, who ran away in 1814, was described as 'fond of playing upon the fiddle' while Abraham's master broadcast that 'he played well on the violin'. A mulatto, offered for sale in 1811, was said to play 'superbly on the tambourine and a little on the fife, beats the drum better than any other in this city, very intelligent, sober and faithful'.

These, among many other references, emphasise that, though the drums were played, the violin and the fife were extremely popular with Negro musicians and slaves within the city of New Orleans half a century before the abolition of slavery. That many – perhaps most – of the slaves mentioned in this period had been imported from Africa seems undeniable and the question inevitably arises whether their fondness for and skill with the violin or simple woodwind owed anything to capacities acquired before enslavement. In these reports the banjo figures much less frequently than the fiddle. 'The banjo', wrote George Washington Cable in the 1880s, 'is not the favourite musical instrument of the Negroes of the Southern States of America. Uncle Remus says truly that this is the fiddle; but for the true African dance . . . there was wanted the dark inspiration of African drums and the banjo's thrump and strum.'

Such a record of Negro fiddles and fiddle players can be echoed throughout the old South, where banjos were also noted at an early date. Nearly two hundred years ago, in May 1774, Nicholas Cresswell from England witnessed a Negro dance in Nanjemoy, Maryland. In his *Journal* he wrote that the Negroes 'generally meet together and amuse themselves with dancing to the Banjo. This musical instrument (if it may be so called) is made of a Gourd something in the imitation of a Guitar with only four strings and played with the fingers in the same manner. Some of them sing to it, which is very droll music indeed. In their songs they generally relate the usage they have received from their Masters or Mistresses in a very satirical manner. Their poetry is like the Music – Rude and uncultivated. Their dancing is most

violent exercise, but so irregular grotesque I am not able to describe it.' Ten years later, Thomas Jefferson in his *Notes on Virginia* endorsed these observations. In music 'they are more generally gifted than the whites, with accurate ears for a tune and time, and they have been found capable of imagining a small catch' he wrote, noting particularly that 'the instrument proper to them is the *banjar*, which they brought thither from Africa.' It seems likely that when, seventy years after, the 'Big Four' of minstrelsy, Dick Pelham, Billy Whitlock, Frank Bower and Dan Emmett, formed The Virginia Minstrels, they did base their performance, for all its caricature, on Negro prototypes. Emmett played the fiddle, Whitlock the four-stringed banjo, Pelham the tambourine and Bower clacked the bones. Though minstrelsy was soon to follow a path which led the native American show far away from Negro music, in these earliest years the dramatic success of the Four may well have related directly to the effectiveness of their mimicry of Negro musicians, playing fiddle, banjo and rhythm instruments.

In the early 1840s, when Dan Emmett and his company were galvanising audiences with their versions of Negro music and jigging, Thomas D. Rice, the originator of *Jim Crow*, sang his ditty and danced the shuffling steps that he had copied from a

Negro stable-hand in Pittsburg. But Fanny Kemble, witnessing a ball on Pierce Butler's plantation in 1839, wrote: 'I have seen Jim Crow – the veritable James; all the contortions, and springs, and flings, and kicks, and capers you have been beguiled into accepting as indicative of him are spurious, faint, feeble, impotent – in a word, pale Northern reproductions of that ineffable black conception.' She was fascinated by the dancing, 'the languishing elegance of some – the painstaking laboriousness of others – above all . . . the feats of a certain enthusiastic banjo player who seemed to me to thump his instrument with every part of his body at once.' In these early days when slaves were still pouring in from Africa – notwithstanding the illegality of the trade – and Africa was a live memory for many on the plantations, reports of plantation customs suggest the persistence of African practices. Kenneth Stampp quotes a report that 'at Christmas in eastern North Carolina, they begged pennies from the whites as they went John Canoeing (or "John Cunering") along the roads, wearing masks and outlandish costumes, blowing horns, tinkling tambourines, dancing and chanting.' He quotes the *Farmers' Register* of 1838 which related a persimmon party among Virginia slaves, where the banjo player had his chair atop a beer barrel and 'a long white cowtail, queued with red ribbon ornamented

Left: The banjo in Thomas Jefferson's day. Below: Dan Emmett (fiddle) and Billy Whitlock (banjo) of the Virginia Minstrels, 1840's.

his head and hung gracefully down his back' and his tricorn hat was decorated with peacock feathers, a rose cockade, a bunch of ripe persimmons' and 'three pods of red pepper as a top-knot'. Slaves, noted Stampp, 'danced to the music of the fiddle or banjo, or they beat out their rhythms with sticks on tin pans or by clapping their hands or tapping their feet' and James Weldon Johnson stated that 'every plantation had its talented band that could

crack jokes, and sing and dance to the accompaniment of the banjo and the "bones"; the bones being actual ribs of sheep or other small animal, cut the proper length, scraped clean and bleached in the sun. When the planter wished to entertain his guests, he needed only to call his troupe of black minstrels.'

Further elaboration is not necessary here, but detailed examination of plantation records and early writings would substantiate the evidence that the fiddle and the banjo were the most prominent of instruments used by the slaves and their immediate successors, with hand-drums, tambourines, bones, rattles made from jawbones of animals, triangles, and fifes, whistles and flutes also often played. Predominating in most accounts are the references to the stringed instruments, which themselves became fundamental to the effectiveness of minstrel-show parodies of Negro music: fiddle and banjo, tambo' and bones. Of course the fiddle was in itself a popular instrument of European immigrants and provided the music for the dance in folk gatherings of the white populace. Among the more devout of the latter, especially the Presbyterian Scots and the Methodists of the Great Awakening, the fiddle was the instrument of the Devil. There could have been relatively little opposition to the playing of the instrument by Negro slaves, whose very blackness would have accorded with the folk image of the fiddler.

Banjo player and fiddler alike developed techniques on their instruments that were copied by white musicians, but the Negro community was sufficiently separate for them to develop traditions which were distinct. Ultimately some elements of these were passed into the blues, even if the guitar, popularised at the close of the nineteenth century, largely replaced them. The sliding notes and *glissandi* of the fiddle were matched upon the guitar strings as fingers pressed them across the frets; the percussive 'thrump and strum' of the banjo was carried on the bass strings by the thumb. These techniques could conceivably have evolved solely on the North American continent, but their singularity suggests that some musical heritage was represented within them which was special to the Negro slave from Africa. But if so, where in those parts of Africa from which the slaves were drawn did such traditions exist? Few writers on jazz and blues – perhaps none – are as familiar with African music as they are with North American Negro music and must therefore depend on the available

A veteran ex-slave banjo-player, photographed 1902.

writings on the former with all their contradictions and perplexities.

Some of the problems that arise may be illustrated by one of the few blues studies to consider the African influence in any detail. In his book, *The Bluesmen*, Samuel Charters notes that the solo song forms of the Ila and Tonga people were 'closely related to the blues that were to develop on another continent more than a century later, not only musically, but also as a concept of an individual song style developing in the midst of a communal music tradition'. After describing them he notes that the widespread 'style of singing was one of the few areas of solo performance within a communal framework in West Africa . . .' In fact, however, the Ila and Tonga people are neither of them West African, but separated by vast terrains, culturally and linguistically, from that region, being of the Middle Zambesi 2,300 miles away. They were a people virtually untouched by the slave trade to the Americas and any links with the blues must therefore be demonstrative both of remarkably common factors in African music and great tenacity of tradition. 'There was also in Africa a strong tradition of guitar-like instruments, and most of the early accompaniment styles in the blues seem to have grown from the rhythmic finger picking styles that had been developed in West Africa' Charters continued. 'The instrument was introduced in Africa by the Portuguese in the fifteenth or sixteenth century in its earliest European form as the small "matchet" or rabequina. Using this

Instruments influenced by European forms are found in many coastal regions. This nsambi, *similar to the* ramkie, *comes from Congo.*

as a model, the African musicians built crude guitars that were called rabekin, ramakienjo, ramakie, rabouquin or ramki.' His source for this data was *The Musical Instruments of the Native Races of South Africa* by Percival R. Kirby. Kirby makes it clear that the ramkie was essentially an instrument of the Cape and quotes O. F. Mentzel who was there between 1733 and 1741 and who gave a detailed description of the instrument. Mentzel stated that the instrument had been brought by slaves from Malabar – Portuguese India – to the Cape and there copied by Hottentot musicians. Other reporters noted the instrument among the Bantu and Bushmen, though Kirby agreed that it was originally developed by the Hottentot. Some 3,000 miles from West Africa it can in no way be associated with the music of that region and had no part to play in the slave trade to North America. This does not, of course, preclude the possibility that the music of the Cape Hottentots is in some way related to that of West Africa – as the xylophones of Madagascar, the Congo, Cameroun or Mali are related – but greatly weakens any argument of direct influence.

Direct influence of the African xylophone on the marimba of the West Indies arises from the frequency with which this instrument is found in the West African countries. But it is inaccurate to say that 'three stringed instruments were common, but most of them had six, as well as the characteristic guitar finger board, sound box, and moveable pegs', and that it was 'clearly an influence on the American musical style', for in fact the remkie is not found in West Africa, six-stringed instruments are unusual even among examples of the ramkie and the characteristic guitar structure is not typical of West African instruments. The strings are usually tuned with adjustable rings, the arm that takes them is usually cylindrical and without frets, and moveable pegs are rare. The arched harp of *Central* Africa had both an approximate hour-glass shape and pegs, but the latter, as Sibyl Marcuse notes, 'are immovable, their purpose being to prevent the strings from slipping'.

Neither the Cape, the Middle Zambesi nor Central Africa had any significant part to play in the provision of slaves for North America. It seems important therefore to consider the music of the regions which did supply the slaves and to examine what relationship it may have to the development of Negro music in the United States in order to have some grounds for speculation on the possible influence it may ultimately have had upon the blues.

MUSIC IN WEST AFRICA

150 miles inland from the coast of Ghana, the bush is dense. According to the vegetation maps, the tropical rain forest thins out in Ghana, and, compared with Sierra Leone or parts of Ivory Coast or Nigeria, is even considered to be non-existent. But to the visitor, even though primal forest probably survives nowhere in the country, the lush vegetation, the huge leaves like elephants' ears, the soaring, unstable cotton trees combine to give an impression of congested and barely tamed growth. Laterite roads, red and hard, raising clouds of choking dust under the wheels of a 'mammy wagon' in the dry season, deeply rutted, saturated and often impassably flooded in the rainy season, wind through the forest. Narrower paths and twisting tracks lead off into the bush to villages of laterite mud houses and thatched markets. From these can be heard the rumble and thunder of the drums through the hours of the night and a soft roar of village voices. Above them, clear and penetrating, the sharp clacking of the 'gong-gong' strikes a persistent, unflagging pattern until daybreak.

Driving through the bush one may happen upon a celebration; more often it can be heard from a distant and hidden village unlocated in the deceptive acoustics of the bush. Occasions like these are often the wakes and successive celebrations which are held at intervals after the death of a member of the community. In Ashanti the number of functions and occasions when the villagers gather for dancing are numerous: puberty festivals, meetings of hunter and warrior associations, religious festivals and cult ceremonials, state assemblies and so on. And there are the social occasions when the *adowa* bands play primarily for recreational purposes. Every function has its special drum orchestras and often the drum groups are named specifically for the one dance or celebration for which they perform a limited number of instrumental pieces. To the untrained ear the complex of rhythms is difficult to disentangle and the total sound from one orchestra may seem very like that of another; to the Ashanti the rhythms are distinct and the conjunction of patterns, the offsetting of the rhythms of the different drums against the gongs and against each other, sets up an exhilarating tension whose complexity he may interpret in his dancing. And, while the rhythm patterns combine to produce a texture of a complexity which defies analysis, the *atumpan*, the 'talking drums', speak the traditional phrases in bursts, intermittent eruptions and rolls of sound intelligible only to those who can hear their language.

The elders sit beneath shelters of palm leaves, while the young men bring crates of locally brewed beer. Flaming orange cloths wrapped round the body with one end thrown over the left shoulder proclaim that this is a funeral. Purple cloths can be seen too, and very occasionally a black one, but it is the great splash of indian red, with the *adinkra* patterns stamped upon them, which gives a brave show of colour to the scene. In the clearing dancers raise small spurts of dust from their sandalled feet as they twist and turn, descend to their knees or leap in the air, to imitate and interpret the occupations and the pleasures of the deceased and themselves. A chorus of women sings in chanting fashion, with one woman leading with vocal lines to which they respond, seemingly without relationship to the compelling rhythms of the *adowa* band. Shaded by an awning, the *adowa* band pours out its rhythms, the two players of the *donno* tension drums standing beside the *atumpan* drummer whose large instru-

An Ashanti adowa *band, (with the* atumpan *'talking drums' seen at the right), playing for a 'fetish dance' to the* obosom *or local god.*

Above: an Ashanti orchestra with the atumpan *and the* donno *tension drums.* Dawuro (*'Banana' gong*) *players in foreground.*

ments are raised before him on a stand. On his left sits the *apen-temma* drummer with his alto drum, and the heavy-sounding *petia* drum is beside him. Behind are the players of the male and female 'gongs', banana-shaped tubes of metal struck with lengths of iron which create a ringing, unvarying rhythmic line against the complex of variations within the strict structure of the instrumental performance. If the excitement of the drumming and the spectacle of the dancing seem contrary to the grief of the bereaved, they find solace in the messages of sympathy addressed to them by the *atumpan* drums.

It was drumming like this which I heard at many functions through the kindness and grave courtesy of the elders and headmen of Ashanti villages. For me it was deeply exhilarating music and the occasions which I was privileged to attend, culminating in a cult or 'fetish' dance for a local *obosom*, or protective spirit, were simple and moving. But when I thought about the music being created here in the heart of the Ashanti region, the centre of slave trading on the Guinea coastal regions, it seemed far, far removed from jazz, still further from the blues. If the slaves came from here, what happened to their music to make so marked a transformation? Or were the slaves brought from other regions by the Ashanti and sold to the white traders at Winneba, or

Sekondi or Bushwa? It seemed important to ascertain which music-producing cultures flourished in Africa and what bearing they could reasonably have on the music of the Deep South.

Alan P. Merriam has identified as distinct musical regions those of the Hottentot-Bushman; East Africa; East Horn; Central Africa; West Coast; Sudan Desert; and the North Coast. Of these the Central African and West Coast regions are 'differentiated from each other perhaps more in terms of degree than of kind', he wrote, 'The West Coast area is distinguished by a strong emphasis on percussion instruments and especially by the use of "hot" rhythm.' The idea of 'hot rhythm' is one which Richard A. Waterman borrowed from jazz and applied to African drumming. In Merriam's view the 'hot' concept 'as well as the traditional use of the three-drum choir and the consistent use of drums in a majority of types of music, extends southward in the coastal regions of French Equatorial Africa and the Belgian Congo', but he points out that it 'seems to be nowhere in Africa as strong as it is along the Guinea Coast'. Merriam, however, questions Waterman's emphasis on 'drums, rattles and gongs' and the dependence of most African instruments on percussion instruments, noting that 'this excludes the large number of string and wind instruments as well as unaccompanied song. It would seem wiser to speak of African *music* as percussive, rather than to emphasize the use of percussion instruments exclusively.'

In the West African region identified by Merriam it is indisputable that the drum orchestra has always played the most important part in the music of the many peoples and tribes that come within its compass. 'We are almost a nation of dancers, musicians, and poets. Thus every great event, such as a triumphant return from battle, or other cause of public rejoicing, is celebrated in public dances, which are accompanied with songs and music suited to the occasion,' wrote the Ibo slave Olaudah Equiano. Born in 1745 he was captured in a slaving expedition in 1756 and taken to Virginia. Later, he was taken to England and sold to Captain Henry Pascal, but he purchased his freedom in 1766. In later years he became an active member of the anti-slavery movement and his 'Interesting Narrative' was published when he was forty-four. He described the dances and the music of his tribe, each representing 'some interesting aspect of real life, such as a great achievement, domestic employment, a pathetic story, or some rural sport; and, as the subject is generally founded on some recent event, it is therefore ever new. This gives our dances a

31

spirit and variety which I have scarcely seen elsewhere. We have many musical instruments, particularly drums of different kinds, a piece of music which resembles a guitar, and another much like a stickado. These last are chiefly used by betrothed virgins, who play them on all grand festivals.' Equiano's description would be quite applicable to the dances and the music of the Akan, whose drumming orchestras play specific pieces of great rhythmic complexity but to which the dancers invent new and descriptive steps. His 'piece of music resembles a guitar' which was probably a chordophone such as is found among most West African coastal tribes, though not with the frequency of the drums.

Between the lands of the Ibo and those of the Ashanti (Akan) of the old Gold Coast (Ghana) lie the domains of the Yoruba of Nigeria and Dahomey, and those of the Ewe of Togoland and eastern Ghana. In these, as well as in the sub-tribes, the drums are of great importance. Their use is not static but shows both evolution and influence. So Anthony King identified the *Igbin* drum family as appropriate for the god Obàtálá; the *Bàta* drum family for the worship of Sàngo, *Ogìdàn* drums to worship Ogun and *Ipèsì* for the god Ifá, yet he observed in *Yoruba Sacred Music* that one drum family, *Dùndún*, 'serve, instead of those previously listed, in the worship of the gods concerned'. This adaptability and eventual dominance of one type may help to indicate how a multitude of drumming practices may have eventually been merged into a few basic ones on transplantation to the Americas, where, as has been noted, Sàngo and Ogun are still worshipped.

Further west among the Ewe, the Reverend A. M. Jones did the field work which led to his important *Studies in African Music*, in which he analysed in detail the structures of the *Nyayito*, *Sovu* and other funeral and ritual dances of the Ewe, with the expert guidance of the master drummer, Desmond Tay. 'Drumming', he contended in *African Rhythm*, 'is the very heart of African music. In it are exhibited all those features of rhythmic interplay wherein African music differs fundamentally from the West.' He identified many salient characteristics: that 'the main beats never coincide', that crossing the beats 'is absolutely fundamental to African music'. These are substantiated in detail by Kwabena Nketia, whose studies of *Drumming in Akan Communities* identify some sixty kinds of drum, more than a score of drum types and many specific functions for which the drum orchestras are indispensable. How pervasive the importance of drumming is, he indicates in

32

Ewe master drummer playing the five-feet long atsimevu. *Directions are given to the orchestra by striking the side of the drum.*

great detail, but the passion for rhythm, drumming and rhythmic dancing of the people is everywhere manifest. 'Arising from the general conditioning for rhythm is a widespread passion for rhythm-making. Boxes, tins, pans, even mortars and pestles may

Above: In West African drumming, fingers, palm and the ball of the thumb are used as well as drum sticks. In the Ewe orchestra the kidi *and* sogo *drums, like the inclined* atsimevu, *are barrel-shaped.*

be turned, especially temporarily, into instruments for rhythm making by young and old. There is usually in these excursions some indication of a grasp of the principles of pitch contrast, phrasing and "crossing of rhythms" that underline Akan drumming.' Between these tribes and the peoples of Dahomey, Togo and the Gold Coast there was influence and contact as the shared instruments, dances and tunings identified by Nketia in his paper, *The History and the Organisation of Music in West Africa*, indicate.

Similar important drum orchestras are to be found throughout the coastal rain forest belts of West Africa as the recordings of Gilbert Rouget, Charles Duvelle and Donald Thurlow among the Baule of Ivory Coast stress. Further details of the drum traditions in the tropical rain forest belt are superfluous, for the evidence of their number and pervasiveness is overwhelming. Comparison of the recordings reveals similarities of approach to rhythm and even, in some instances, similar rhythm patterns. Generally the master drum carries the burden of rhythmic complexity and the supporting drums, graded in size, pitch and tone, set up rhythms against it and each other. 'The crossing of the beat *must* be established; after that is done, additional drums may be added with main beats of the bar coinciding with one or other of those already beating', Father Jones has explained, 'but with a different rhythm-pattern; or, in the case of the master drum, once the first two drums have established a cross-rhythm, he may do just what he likes; he usually creates a series of rhythm-patterns whose main beat crosses at least one of the other drums.' Professor Nketia has pointed out that the rhythms are conceived either unilineally with the patterns 'assigned to one drum or a pair of drums played by one man, or to many drums played by different men. In the latter case, a number of the same type of drum or different drums may be playing the particular set of rhythms together'; or multilineally, where 'a number of rhythm patterns are assigned to two or more drums, each drum or group of drums beating different patterns or adopting different sequences of patterns in such a way as to offset some beats of their respective patterns.' Against these may be placed hand-claps, often by two or three individuals or groups of people, whose clap rhythms are also played against each other, while the 'gongs' or clapperless bells establish a metronomic time signal. The suggestion that the master drummer may 'do just what he likes' is rather misleading, for the length and character of the rhythm phrases is determined by the function, the nature of the dance and the 'piece' that is being performed. Improvisation, in fact, is very strictly controlled. As Nketia has pointed out in a paper on the music of the Ga people, 'the drummers of an ensemble cannot just drum what catches their fancy. They have to know what is required of them in respect of rhythm and tone. They have to know the basic parts assigned to each drum and how they are intended to be combined.

For although the resources of drums are limited, they can be arranged in different ways so as to produce drum pieces which can be clearly distinguished from each other.'

To what extent is the West African approach to drum music and its rhythms reflected in jazz and the blues ? To Harold Courlander, the links are direct. 'There is no doubt,' he said, 'that drums were widely used in the African manner in the United States as late as seventy or eighty years ago. Literature on Louisiana is prolific with references to drums. A survey conducted in the Sea Islands of Georgia only a relatively few years ago produced evidence that persons then alive recalled the use of drums for dances and death rites. In Alabama in 1950 I found the remains of an old peg-type drum being used as a storage container for chicken feed. It is probable that the persistent use of the shallow tambourine or finger drum by certain Negro groups stems as much from African tradition as from European. In secular folk music, the wash-tub bass is played precisely in the manner of the African earth bow: the string is plucked and beaten by one player, while a second beats on the inverted tub as though it were a drum.' Harold Courlander has likewise compared the drum battery of Baby Dodds with aspects of African usage. 'Different tones are produced on the block by striking it in different spots and with different parts of the drumstick, as in the case of the African slit-log drum. The left-hand "hard" beats are called "mama" and the right-hand "soft" beats are called "daddy" 'and he compares this with West Indian and West African terminology. Yet it must be acknowledged that, whatever the links with African drumming, and they may not be as numerous as this suggests, conceptually jazz music is very different.

To the ear accustomed to both jazz and African music, it is apparent that the fundamental opposition of rhythms and the multilinear rhythmic approach of African drumming is only marginally echoed in American jazz. Though Waterman has emphasised the 'hot' character of the drumming of both cultures, jazz does not get its impetus from the use of cross-rhythms, except in so far as the trombone, trumpet or clarinet may be said to be used rhythmically. The 'rhythm section' is controlled heavily by the 'beat' and this allows none of the tension to develop which is characteristic of the drum orchestras of the African rain forests. Instead, jazz developed a different kind of rhythmic feeling with a lifting movement between adjacent beats which the jazz musician identifies as 'rock' or 'swing.' Waterman relates this to the 'metronome sense': 'Musical terms like "rock" and "swing" express ideas of rhythm foreign to European folk tradition, and stem from African concepts, as does the extremely basic idea of the application of the word "hot" to musical rhythms. The development of a "feeling for the beat", so important in jazz musicianship, is neither more nor less than the development of the metronome sense.' But, if this is so, then nearly all the other African concepts of rhythm were discarded in its favour, for in the jazz sense, West African drum orchestras simply do not 'swing'. The 'ride' of a New Orleans jazz band, the 'slow and easy' slow-drag of a country blues band, have no counterpart in the forceful thrust of the multilineal drum rhythms.

In jazz drumming the most African-seeming characteristic of its rhythms lies in the shifting of accents to the weak or 'off'-beats – syncopation in fact. But syncopation of this kind is not an element of African drumming, and only appears so through the filter of western notation. 'Any attempt to write African music in the European manner,' wrote Father Jones, 'with bar lines running right down the score and applying to all the contributing instruments simultaneously, is bound to lead to confusion. It gives the impression that all but one of the contributors is highly syncopated, and the multitude of tied notes and off-beat accents makes the mind reel. Looked at from the point of view of each player, African music is not syncopated nor is it complicated except for the master-drum rhythms.'

In addition to those problems which arise from the relation of the jazz approach in rhythm and syncopation to the West African concepts of drumming, there are similar difficulties stemming from the use of wind instruments and the nature of jazz improvisation. Though horns are used in parts of the rain forest, they are seldom employed with the drum orchestras and have relatively little flexibility. Improvisation on the theme, which is fundamental to jazz, also appears to owe little to improvisation within tight rhythmic patterns on the drums.

All these problems are present in a still more marked degree when the blues is considered. Largely a vocal music, it is also one which was, in its formative years, created by solo artists, or by pairs of musicians. The 'blues band' is seldom of more than four of five pieces at any event, and even when it is as large as this it is dominated by stringed instruments. Blues singers working solo with a guitar or with a piano are in the majority; combinations of two guitars, guitar and mandolin, or guitar and piano are fairly

The Mobile Strugglers, country blues band near Montgomery, Alabama employed two fiddles, guitar, plucked bass, and tub bass doubling on mandolin-banjo. They played for dances and 'slow-drags'.

common; while guitar and fiddle, guitar and harmonica or, occasionally, piano and harmonica have all been popular in varying degrees. The use of string and tub basses, washboards, and jugs, with the rare survival of banjo and the infrequent use of the kazoo, more or less rounds out the customary use of instruments in the blues. When blues instrumentation, improvisation, rhythm and use of vocals are compared with the music of the rain forest drum orchestras they seem even further removed than jazz from this African tradition. It was precisely because of these considerations that the music of Kunaal and Sosira in the village of Nangodi seemed so important to me. For here was the combination of vocal, rhythm and stringed instrument which hinted at a link with the blues; here, too, I heard in person for the first time an African music which could be said to 'swing' in the jazz sense, where the singer and his accompanist seemed free to improvise and where the combination of instruments had a certain feeling of syncopation.

Sosira and Kunaal represented a different tradition in African music, and though they were on the southern fringe of it they were related to a body of song and musical expression which extended in a great belt across the sub-Saharan savannah regions.

Although they are all of them Negro peoples, the tribes that inhabit this vast region are, in many ways, distinct from those of the rain forest. The history is complicated by the movement of peoples during the past five centuries, but certain generalisations can be made which are substantiated by linguistic evidence. Although virtually all the tribes of West Africa south of the Senegal River may be considered as speaking Sudanic languages, they may be grouped into major divisions which have been most exhaustively examined by Joseph H. Greenberg. Though some details are disputed, in general his African linguistic classification is accepted by scholars and may be briefly summarised. The coastal rain forest tribes, of which the Ashanti are a federation, come within the Kwa group which stretches from Liberia east to Ibo territory in Nigeria. Within this belt are included the Baule, Twi, (Ashanti), Ewe, Yoruba and Ibo speaking peoples. North of them are the Gur group, taking in the Bobo, Mossi and Dogon peoples among many others, while to the north-west is the massive group of Manding or Mande speaking peoples, including the Malinke, (Mandingo), Bambara and Soninke. Along the coast

Chicago street band photographed by Big Bill Broonzy about 1937. It included guitar, banjo and tub bass with broomhandle.

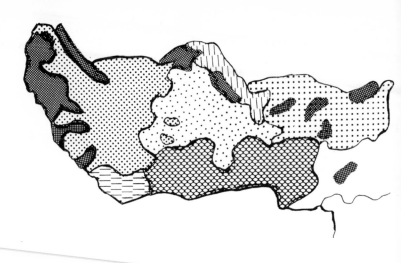

WEST AFRICA – *Linguistic areas*

(adapted from J. H. Greenberg and others)

 West Atlantic: includes Wolof, Serer, Diola, Temne, and Fulani (the Fulani are pastoral–nomadic).

Mande (Mandingo): includes Soninke, Malinke, Mende, Vai, Kpele, Dan, Guere, Bambara, and Dyoula.

 Kru: small region including Kru, Grebo, and Bakwe.

Gur: includes Senufo, Lobi, Dagomba, Grunshi, Gurensi, Mossi, Dogon, and Gurma. (With pockets of Mande Dyoula.)

 Kwa: includes Baule, Anyi, Ashanti, Fanti, Ga, Brong, Yoruba, Nupe, and Ibo.

 Songhai.

Chado-Hamitic: includes Hausa, Sokoto, Bede, Ngizim. (Tuareg are Berber, penetrating from the north. Also pockets of Fulani.)

from Senegal to Liberia are to be found the west Atlantic sub-family which includes the Wolof, Dyola and the scattered groups of the Fulani.

Apart from the Kru speaking peoples of Liberia, it will be seen that the peoples of the drum orchestras are within the Kwa group. This is partly due to the vegetation, which is dense tropical forest yielding large-boled woods suitable for the making of big drums. As one moves north from the rain forest and into the tropical woodlands and savannah mosaic regions, the trees become fewer and smaller. They are less suitable to the making of drums and are prized, when they do grow large, for the shade they offer. Further north still, the savannah parklands give way to steppe and eventually, to the desert. In the savannah regions the woods available for instruments are small-boled and they are more frequently fashioned into resonators for stringed instruments, or into strips for xylophones. But in these regions calabashes and gourds grow, providing other types of resonator, and the bodies for large calabash drums.

For many centuries the savannah and grassland peoples have been assailed by Muslims from the north, so that many of them have totally embraced Islam. Others have partially retained their pagan animism, while some tribes are divided between pagan and Muslim groups. To the south on the other hand, along the rain forest, the peoples have been exposed to Christianity and western missionaries, while their tribal religions are strongly animistic and in some cases, the Yoruba for instance, have a pantheon of gods. Contact with Islam has affected the savannah peoples culturally in a number of ways, the Muslim strictures against representational arts, for instance, resulting in sculpture that is more abstract in form than the more figurative sculptures of the rain forest; many of the Manding-speaking tribes produce little sculpture at all. Of course, the available woods again affect the artifacts, savannah sculptures tending towards 'pole' forms, while those of the rain forest are more fully realised in the round. The vegetation and climate also affect the crops; millet is the staple diet among the savannah peoples, yams and tree crops are staples in the coastal belt. Ethnically, the peoples are complex, but those on the coast include a large proportion with high counts of the sickle-cell gene making them resistant to malaria and able to withstand heat and high humidity; those in the savannah belt include large numbers of tribes with low sickle-cell counts and lower resistance to malaria, yet they are physically more suited to a dry atmosphere, high day temperatures and cool nights.

North of the rain forest there stretches a belt of savannah and semi-desert some 250 miles in depth and sweeping from Lake Chad in the interior eastwards for nearly 2,000 miles. It takes in the northern part of Nigeria, and the southern part of Niger; dips over Dahomey and Togo to take in part of Ghana; embraces the Republic of Upper Volta and the southern part of the Federation of Mali; and takes in the north of Guinea to Gambia and Senegal on the west Atlantic coast. Within this great belt live hundreds of tribes who are linguistically, culturally, climatically and environmentally distinct from the Kwa-speaking peoples of the coastal rain forest, even though they are all Negro and all speaking Sudanic languages. It is the latter (Kwa) who have been the subject of comparative studies concerning African retentions on jazz and the music of the Negro in the Americas: the drum-dominated tribes of the Ashanti, Yoruba and Ewe. North of them are peoples who also have drums and who also employ drum orchestras, but among whom are to be found a variety of stringed instruments, horns, flutes and xylophones, which together reveal a broader base to the African musical heritage. Is it to these regions that any African retentions in jazz can be traced? And, bearing in mind the combinations of lutes, harps and fiddles, are there any links with the blues and its antecedents to be found here?

It is probably true to say that nearly all African peoples have stringed instruments of some kind, but in those of the tropical rain forest they generally play a very small part in the musical expression of the people. The 'musical bow' which is the ordinary hunting bow plucked as a musical instrument, is to be found in most hunting societies, and there is a curious combination of bows, where each string has a separate stem, that together make the so-called 'West African harp'. Belly-harps and belly-lyres, with single strings held in tension across a bow fitted with a gourd resonator, are also frequently found. With the cup of the resonator placed against the stomach, they can be played by plucking or with a bow-string. Lyres are common, with the horns carrying a cross-piece to which the strings are attached, but monochords plucked, bowed or picked with a plectrum, and similar chordophones with two, three or more strings are even more familiar. In addition there are large harps and plucked lutes; some of the former, with as many as a score of strings on which extremely complex music can be played, are to be found in the western parts of the savannah

42

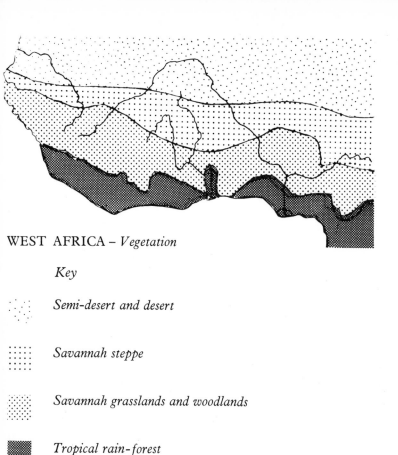

WEST AFRICA – *Vegetation*

Key

Semi-desert and desert

Savannah steppe

Savannah grasslands and woodlands

Tropical rain-forest

regions. To the ear attuned to blues it is the manner of playing that impresses, with the moaned and wailing notes of the bowed instruments, the rapid fingering of the lutes and harps, and the combined interweaving of melodic-rhythmic lines when two or more musicians play together, offering some remarkable comparisons. The pentatonic and heptatonic scales often used by many of the savannah peoples do not preclude the inflections and shadings that come from rising to hit the notes, relaxing tension on the strings, or drawing the bow across them to make immediate parallels with the 'blue notes' – diminished thirds and sevenths – familiar in blues and jazz.

In the African countries where Islam has had a powerful influence and where chiefs exert considerable authority, much of the music-making is the province of the *griots*. These are traditional musicians who are employed as individuals, or in pairs, or even in very large groups and orchestras. In many savannah societies the *griots* are professional musicians, but in some – as in Senegal – they are part-time entertainers and may also be farmers, fishermen or follow some other occupation. The latter may be attached to a village and may have only a small, local reputation

as song makers and instrumentalists, but in many regions the *griots* are employed by the sultans, emirs, chiefs or headmen. Others – the most famous – are free-ranging groups of professional musicians, unattached to any employer, who hire their services out to families, groups of workers or others who wish to hear and temporarily employ them. Many *griots* were slaves at one time and some, technically, still are. But the freely travelling, nomadic *griots* are totally independent and proud of it. 'The musical arts of the *griots*,' wrote Tolia Nikiprowetzky when introducing a collection of their recordings in Niger, 'is rich and varied. The basis of their repertoire consists of songs of praise: the *griot* is attached to a chief and by custom flaunts the qualities of his master and perpetuates the memory of the members of his family who have preceded him in his ruling functions, or have singled themselves out by their efforts. When attached to a "professional body" (cultivators, fishermen, butchers, etc.) the *griot* praises the achievements of some members of the profession and encourages the efforts of the workers.' The *griots* play for important occasions like marriages, circumcisions and the like, and leave with considerable sums of money. It is stated that one celebrated *griot* in Senegal has a more substantial income than the highest-paid officials in the country.

Generally, indeed almost invariably, the *griots* are the sons and nephews of older *griots*, their role being hereditary. They are taught by their fathers and uncles and are trained over many years to learn the enormous quantity of traditional songs and to master the melodies and rhythms which are expected of them. A *griot* is required to sing on demand the history of a tribe or family for seven generations and, in particular areas, to be totally familiar with the songs of ritual necessary to summon spirits and gain the sympathy of the ancestors. Some of the *griots* are women, though they are generally the wives of the male singers, and they gather gossip and details which the *griot* may incorporate into his songs. For though he has to know many traditional songs without error he also must have the ability to extemporise on current events, chance incidents and the passing scene. Their wit can be devastating and their knowledge of local history formidable. As Curt Sachs noted, 'they importune the rich with either glorification or insults depending on whether their victims are open-handed or stingy. They often roam from village to village in gangs of about

Left: typical harp-lute and belly-harps of the savannah region.

a dozen under a chief who is at the same time a seasoned historian and genealogist and knows to the last details the alliances, hostilities and conflicts that unite or oppose the families and villages of the country.' This puts the *griots* in a position of some power; they blackmail their listeners with their ridicule and are feared and despised for it, while being admired for their skill. The attitude of their audiences is ambivalent, for while they fear being the butt of their humour they want to hear the gossip and news they purvey, and listen to their music.

Arabic has been adopted by the learned among the cultures of the savannah regions and the Muslim schools have brought a degree of literacy. But it is primarily an oral culture and hence the *griot* plays an important role within it. He has a stock-in-trade of songs and words, he has a standard available repertoire of tunes, but he is also an innovator and a manipulator. He fits new words to old musical themes, models old phrases into new ideas, and rather than being a perpetuator of attitudes is, as Nikiprowetzky has pointed out, in Senegal at any rate, an instrument for social change. Nevertheless, these are slowly moving societies and the *griots* have been established for many centuries, and may well continue to be. Their position in the society is an ambiguous one: both privileged and un-privileged. They can acquire large fortunes and as the custom of giving and receiving gifts is prevalent among savannah peoples, with 'giving' gathering the higher esteem, the *griot* is often the recipient of gifts from his master. But they are a caste apart, as André Jolivet has explained, 'the last in the hierarchy with the smiths, the rope-makers and the weavers'. Among many tribes who venerate the earth and whose ancestors are intimately associated with them, the interment of a *griot* would be a desecration. Instead of being buried, therefore, their bodies are placed upright in the trunks of hollow baobab trees and allowed to putrefy.

In the pursuit of the profession, many *griots* achieve remarkable standards of virtuosity. The players of the great harp-lute, called the *kora*, for instance, combine melodic inventiveness with subtls and constantly moving rhythms, plucking the twenty-one stringe of their instrument with the thumbs, while steadying their hands on two projecting wood horns. Or they may play a ground bass and play intricate patterns over it while singing in a third layer a

Left: Soudioulou Sissoko from the Casamance of Senegal, playing the twenty-one string kora, *which originated in Guinea.*

praise song, or improvised market-place satire. Among the Mandingo sub-tribe of the Malinke, the *seron*, a variant of the *kora* with nineteen strings, is equally popular, while in the Gambia, the *bulumbata* offers a further variant. Made like the others from a huge calabash and covered with a skin, it has a curving arm which carries the strings and which terminates in a metal plate festooned with rings that vibrate with every touch of the strings. These instruments have their strings held in place by tuning rings, or leather loops, which are slid when wet up the shaft of the arm and allowed to tighten on drying.

Some bands of *griots* comprise a large number of musicians, singers and praise-shouters – sometimes as many as twenty. But five or six is more usual and trios, or pairs, of musicians very common. In the larger orchestras there are many kinds of instrument; or alternatively there are those which have a large assembly of a single type – drums or horns – which are played for particular functions only. Some of the techniques employed are unusual, such as the calabash drum whose tones are constantly varied by piling up or clearing sand away from the bowl which is half immersed in it. Others show the borrowings of instrumental techniques from nearby peoples: the floating calabashes of the Tuareg for example. Rhythms are important in the music of the *griots*, but, as Nikiprowetzky has observed, 'Contrary to the usual belief that African music is above all rhythm and percussion, we have observed "melody lines" which spontaneously spring to life and unfold according to their own internal nature without being subjected to any rhythmic straightjacket.' It is hard to generalise about a musical culture and tradition which is shared by so many tribes over so vast a region. The *griots'* orchestras are numerous and there is evidence of their increasingly widening influence.

Writing in 1931, William Seabrook noted the presence of *griots* among the Dan and Guere of the Ivory Coast rain forest. 'These are a special class' he wrote, 'and divide further into two separate specialized functions. One type of *griot* is like the subsidized poet or minstrel who was attached to a European Court in the Middle Ages. He is an improvising singer, shouter, orator, whose duty is to flatter and glorify his master. The second type of *griot* corresponds even more precisely to the medieval king's jester. He is a comic fellow to whom every outrageous licence is permitted.' His reports and photographs reveal that the *griots* did not accompany themselves on stringed instruments, or apparently on any musical instrument at all. Thirty years later, Hugo Zemp explained that, in general, any Dan might play an instrument and that 'any one of the boys can learn to play the drum or transverse trumpet. In contrast to these non-professionals, the musicians of the Malinke (the neighbouring tribe in the North) belong to a professional caste of musicians. Some of these *griots* have settled with the Dan and live near the headmen as musicians and leather workers.' Contact with the Malinke was evident in other ways: 'The Northern Dan of the Savannah have adopted the Malinke practice of maintaining permanent hunting groups, and also the musical instrument which the hunters take with them, the *ko* (hunter's harp). This instrument has six or seven strings, arranged in two parallel rows.' Hugo Zemp also found the six-stringed harp-lute among the Senufo whose lands are in the savannah region. They had 'undoubtedly taken over the harp-lute from their Western neighbours, the Malinke. Among the latter it is called *koni* and played by hunters, also to the accompaniment of iron rasps'. Though the Senufo hunters wore similar attire and played rasps 'on no occasion known to us was the principal singer able to play the harp-lute. However the instrument is always carried about and although never sounded, and perhaps for this very reason, has a special significance for the singer.'

Further west among the Wolof of Senegal and Gambia the *griots*, known as the *gewel*, occupy a lowly social position, as Sachs has observed. Their status is below that of the descendants of the slaves of blacksmiths and leather workers and the praise-singers, minstrels, jesters and musicians, and the descendants of their slaves (*jam i gewel*) 'are regarded in some ways as untouchables: they cannot be buried in the village graveyard, and members of other classes will not eat with them out of the same dish'. But, wrote David Ames, 'despite the pretence of laziness presented to the public for business purposes, most of the *gewel* are hard-working farmers and entertainers. They take pride in their artistic abilities, and virtuosos among them are recognized by the whole community and often have a reputation beyond it.' Drums are used by the Wolof; these, however, are not made by them but by Fulbe woodcarvers. Among string instruments the most frequently employed and one of the most favoured of all Wolof instruments is the five-stringed *halam*. A hollowed wood body has hide stretched over it to form a resonator and the strings are fixed by leather tuning thongs to the rounded neck and stretched over a bridge on the resonator. 'The strings are plucked by the fingernail of the thumb, forefinger and the middle finger of the

Above: two griots *playing a* halam *duet. The* halam *has five strings and is considered to be a precursor of the American banjo.*

right hand, and the *gewel* keep their fingernails long for this purpose. Occasionally all of the fingers are used to strike the resonator as in *flamenco* guitar-playing. The two longest strings are stopped with the fingers of the left hand without the aid of frets. The three shorter strings are not stopped but are left "open" and are plucked in constant pitch', Ames has explained, understandably hazarding the guess that the *halam* 'may have been the "grandfather" of the American banjo'. A similar African lute with a gourd bowl also employed in Senegal has, too, been considered to be the source of Jefferson's '*banjar*'. Known as the *bania*, as Curt Sachs has noted in *Reallexikon der Musikinstrumente*, not only its form but even its name may have been transported to North America. Certainly it is not hard to believe that the tradition which shaped the music of the *halam* and the *bania* was the progenitor of the music of such teams as Frank Stokes and Dan Sane or the Georgia Browns, when listening to two professional *gewel* each playing the *halam* in a rapidly moving, cross-rhythmic performance.

1,500 miles to the east of the Senegambia, in the Hausa regions of northern Nigeria, instruments of a similar kind are played for *bori* rituals and ceremonies and on the hunt. The *komo* is a two-stringed lute with a bowl made sometimes out of a calabash, sometimes out of a section of hollowed wood like the *halam*. A strip of metal with vibrating rings inserted around it is to be found on one *komo* in my possession; another has no vibrator.

These instruments are played with a pick or plectrum of rhinocerous hide and are found deep in the Republic of Niger where groups of as many as six *griots* play extremely large instruments, some nearly two metres long, called *garaya*. Among the Hausa of Nigeria the *kukuma* fiddle is also used to accompany praise songs. Horsehair is laid in a band to provide a single 'string' and the instrument is played with a long horsehair bow. Groups of musicians also play a larger form, the *goge*, while in Niger the *goge* (or *gogué*) is played by both solo singers and bands of *griots*. Though the distribution map of these instruments is complex, and the variations of the lutes and fiddles may have differing numbers of strings, like the long-armed *gouroumi* of Niger with its three strings but marked proportional similarity to the banjo, their widespread use over many countries and thousands of miles of savannah territory is without question.

Across the savannah belt drum orchestras among the *griots*, using drums for weddings, funerals and other ceremonies, for the

Below: griots *from the Republic of Niger, part of an orchestra of eleven. Six musicians played the* garaya, *a two-stringed lute with a long resonator, and five played percussion calabash rattles. With this large group there was also a chorus of women singers.*

praise of the chiefs and to accompany particular forms of work, are common, even if they are not as prevalent as in the rain forest. Tension drums, large calabash drums and small drums of skins stretched across potsherds are all to be found. But trumpets and horns are also found in many *griot* orchestras and in the bands maintained by the chiefs, headmen and emirs. The long Hausa trumpet, the *kakaki*, the so-called single reed oboe known as the *algaita* and many other kinds of horn with flat disc mouthpieces, slender reeds, bodies of wood or bamboo and bells of tin or other metal are widely distributed. Much has been written of the 'talking drums' of the Ashanti and the Yoruba with the assumption made that in some way the vocalising techniques have been transferred to wind instruments in the Americas. It would seem that the influence could have been far more direct with a clear retention of savannah practice. Tolia Nikiprowetzky has drawn attention to the virtuosity of the players of the Béri-Béri *algaita* who are able with 'an ingenious system of phonetic equivalents to transmit virtual messages which the initiated can translate with ease'. The Béri-Béri of Niger use similar instruments to the Hausa who employ the use of 'talking' techniques widely. David Ames recorded a Fanfare for the Sultan of Sokoto who is 'senior to all the Emirs and appropriately his musicians are the most expert and proud of all the court musicians'. The court orchestra included three *kakaki* long trumpets, three *algaita*, two double membrane drums with snares (*gangan na sarki*) and five medium length horns of the *farai* type. 'Though there is no singing, all the instruments are "talking",' Ames emphasised. On wind instruments it is possible for imitations to approximate the sounds of speech and song, but this is only practicable on the drums with 'pitch and tone' languages like Twi (Ashanti) or Yoruba. As Wolof is not a tone language the members of the Wolof tribe do not use this technique, and neither do other language groups which do not share this characteristic, though some employ communicative rhythms much as a bugler may sound a 'reveille', or a drummer sound 'retreat'.

Right: Lobi musicians from Lawra. Two men play the gil, *the Lobi fourteen-key xylophone. Beneath the keys may be seen the gourd resonators with spider's egg mirlitons showing as white patches. Other musicians are playing the* dale *earthenware drums,* pira *castanets and a vertical peg drum. Western clothes are worn but the Lobi favour their traditional loose, indigo-striped smock.*

SAVANNAH SONG

Far to the north-west of Ghana where the Black Volta divides the country from the southward dipping finger of Upper Volta, live the Lobi. They have moved from further north at some time and their houses are of a kind most suited to the arid regions of the Sudan. Settling along the Black Volta, where seasonal rains can damage mud-built compounds, they have devised means to adjust to the somewhat more variable climate of the savannah parkland. Their compounds are of rounded buildings, or rectangular huts with rounded corners, and the roofs, with low mud walls, become areas for drying crops and for communication across the compound. When a man builds a house he gets his companions to throw mud balls up to the level where he lays them on the wall. It is hot work in the sun and to make it easier and assist with the rhythms of throwing, catching and laying the balls of mud, a group of musicians plays nearby.

Their principal instrument is the African *balafon*, or xylophone, called a *gil* by the Lobi, and a group may have two, three or even more xylophones. The long strips of hardwood are laid on a sling suspended within a frame structure which stands on the ground before the player. Beneath the slats, which are bevelled until they are tuned correctly, are suspended gourds to amplify the sound.

Above: the singer with the Lobi orchestra.

Most of the gourds have patches of white on their surfaces –
membranes of a spider's egg which are used to seal holes made
in the gourd. Some of the holes are made by termites, but many
of them are deliberately made to achieve refinements of tuning,
for the Lobi have a refined ear for the qualities of sound which
they expect from the *gil*. On occasion two or even more musicians
may play the same xylophone, striking from opposite sides or
playing a rhythm pattern on the end key. When the melodic-
rhythmic patterns of several *gils* and musicians are flowing freely,
a complex of rippling instrumental lines creates an enchanting
sound. In support are two small drums – *dale* – made from the
necks of broken pots over which snake-skins have been stretched.
The drums are played with the fingers and gripped between the
knees of the player; the sound is surprisingly crisp and loud. A
kor, or stem based drum with a goatskin head, provides the bass
rhythm and any number of bystanders may join in by clacking
pira, or iron finger castanets. The musicians do not sing; in this
they resemble the Ashanti *adowa* bands, though there is little
similarity in other respects. Instead, the singing is carried by a
leader whom the orchestra supports. When I recorded a group of

Lobi musicians from Lawra, the singer was a powerfully built man with a string of plastic beads round his neck and a strong, strained voice. Most of his songs were *shebre*, a general term for a song type used for marriages, festivals, harvest ceremonies and other occasions of feasting and celebration. His words were uttered rapidly and he often broke into shrill ululations and shrieks.

What, I wondered, had happened to the *gil*? The Lobi, or those who had previously occupied their territory would have been easily accessible to slave raiders from Ashanti; did any go to the United States and did they bring the *gil* with them? Of course the Lobi *gil* was only one of the many kinds of xylophone to be found right across Africa, spreading across West Africa as far as Guinea. If there is little evidence of Lobi tribesmen in the south, there is evidence enough of Bambara and Malinke (Mandingo), both of which have important traditions with the *balafon*. Was the marimba, the xylophone, ever brought to North America? And what happened to the unique gapped heptatonic scale of the marimba which Father A. M. Jones has shown is essential to the instrument and displays its Oceanic origins?

It may be, as Mack McCormick has suggested, that the lack of the appropriate hardwoods caused the disappearance of the instrument, whereas in mahogany-growing countries further south it has survived. But strips of bamboo and other woods could have been used; perhaps it was simply that the stringency of American slave ownership did not permit the slaves time to make the instrument; the time necessary to fashion a modest *bania* would have been far less. Again, it may have been simply that the piano was available for talented slaves who might perform on a keyboard instrument. It would certainly seem that the combination of repeated rhythm patterns and rhythmic-melodic patterns set against them, such as are characteristic of boogie-woogie and blues piano, is a fairly logical extension of the elements of *balafon* playing. But this does not explain the time-lag that apparently exists before such a pianistic equivalent emerged; perhaps no explanation can be reached.

Undoubtedly the *balafon* has a long history, and its music continually fascinated European travellers and traders to the savannah region. 'When the king had seated his visitors in state before his palace, one of the court musicians – a *griot* as they were called – gave a concert on the *ballafeu*. Of all the strange instruments that the Europeans heard resounding across the Gambia, the *ballafeu*, or xylophone, was the one which most impressed them, both its tones and its ingenious construction,' Professor Douglas Grant has noted, instancing William Smith whose *A New Voyage to Guinea* was published in 1745. 'Smith was so struck by it that he sketched the musician squatting cross-legged before his instrument striking the wooden keyboard with his padded sticks.' But even if the traders were impressed, they seem to have suppressed the instrument in North America even though it became popular in Latin American countries. Suppression of the *balafon* may also have been caused through suspicion that, like the drums, it could be used as a means of communication and therefore as incitement to insurrection. Mungo Park had noted that the drum was applied at wrestling matches 'to keep order among the spectators, by imitating the sound of certain Mandingo sentences: for example, when the wrestling match is about to begin the drummer strikes what is understood to signify *ali boe see*, – sit all down; ... and when the combatants are to begin, he strikes *amuta, amuta*, – take hold, take hold.' Conceivably it was recognised that what was transmittable on the Mandingo drum was also communicable on the Mandingo *balafon*. But it seems more likely that the instrument declined in North America because it was not encouraged and neither the making nor the use had the sanction of the slave-owners. Like the great traditions of African wood sculpture which were shared by innumerable tribes of the slave-producing regions, not excluding the savannah – the Bambara are among the most gifted of sculptors and smiths in West Africa – the *balafon* music withered away with scarcely a trace.

If instrumental skills were encouraged, as in the case of the playing of the fiddle and the banjo, or discouraged as in the instances of the drums and perhaps the xylophones and horns, the natural skills requiring no musical instrument were free to flourish and be developed. The hand-clapping which accompanied musical performances in all parts of West Africa persisted in the Negro church; it was noted as early as the eighteenth century and remained a familiar characteristic of the services of the 'Sanctified' and 'Pentecostal' churches. In the 'thirties it was still far from uncommon for witnesses to report a 'ring-shout' – a shuffling dance in counter-clockwise direction performed by a circle of worshippers which gradually intensified in tempo and collective excitement. In form and character it appears to have been close to the circular dances performed throughout West Africa. Dr Lorenzo Turner even identified the term 'shout' as being identical with the Arabic *saut* used by West African Muslim peoples to mean walking round the *Kaaba*. However, neither hand-clapping nor the ring dance are particularly associated with the blues. On occasions blues singers and audiences will clap on the off-beat, and 'slow-dragging' couples may be seen to be shuffling in a manner reminiscent, perhaps, of the 'shout'. But neither could be said to be characteristic.

Common to most Negro folk music forms in the United States is the vocal. It is not a feature of ragtime, and it is a moot point whether ragtime, with its self-conscious composition, has more than the faintest echoes of African retentions anyway. The vocal is more important in New Orleans jazz, though the emphasis on the use of vocal intonation, in trumpet, cornet and trombone playing in particular, has possibly robbed the earliest jazz bands of singing of special quality, allowing certain exceptions. Any African retentions in the vocal blues would appear to have arisen from a different tradition than that of jazz.

Undoubtedly the strongest vocal tradition extending to the very roots of slavery lies in the work-song. The distribution of work-song patterns in West Africa has yet to be plotted, but it must be strongly affected by the nature of the crops and produce grown. Work songs by a group of workers engaged in the applications of identical labour are mainly to be found in agricultural and farming communities. In the rain forest regions where cocoa, coffee or bananas are grown, the work involved requires less collective labour than does the hoeing, digging or planting of fields. Work songs of a collective kind are therefore less characteristic of the forest regions of western Nigeria, Dahomey, Ashanti or Ivory Coast where cocoa, bananas and coffee are grown. In the tropical grassland or savannah regions, guinea corn, millet and peanuts are among the principal crops and in these regions collective work songs are heard, frequently sung to the accompaniment of small orchestras of strings, rattles and hand drums. They are often intermittent and have less of the organised structure of the North American work songs, with whistles, shouts and calls breaking up their sequence against the regularity of the work. David Sapir recorded examples of the work songs of the Diola-Fogny of the Basse Casamance, the south-western section of Senegal, and has written: 'A Diola usually works his peanut fields by himself or with the aid of a brother or son. But there are certain times when the men of a village quarter work in common cultivating the fields of an elder or earning, for the entire quarter, either money or cattle. Singing is always a part of such communal cultivation.' When a field has been cleared for digging the men line up in a row with as many as fifty preparing to dig. 'It is at this time that the men sing, all together and in rhythm to the digging, interjecting shouts of encouragement and blasts from European-made whistles.' The singing is extemporaneous, in a manner which the Diola have derived from the Mandingos. 'There is a tremendous amount of repetition in the words. However it is just this repetition that allows the singer to go on indefinitely.' In group singing, phrases are sung collectively in chorus and this feature is developed in the songs for rice cultivation. 'Instead of extemporaneous singing, the workers group into two antiphonal choruses to sing songs to set words. A song is repeated over and over again until someone breaks in with a new melody to be taken up by the two choruses.'

In communities where grain is cultivated, the women generally sing over the grinding stones. Their songs are often directed to other women grinding corn with them or in the vicinity. An example recorded by David Ames of a corn-grinding song by Hausa wives in Zaria is typical. 'The number of verses is determined by the quantity of corn to be ground and obviously many are improvised,' Ames explained, his subject satirising or praising other women. 'She boasts that girls living in certain wards of Zaria city are the best dressed, the most competent sexually and are so "thorny" that it is a mistake to trifle with them.' Such work songs are to be found in all parts of Africa where co-ordinated labour is required or where the rhythm of the work itself gives the basis for song. All the same, the farming communities provide the most notable examples. Even in these the singing is not always contributed by the workers, however. Very often an orchestra, a small band of *griots* or a group of professional musicians, may play for the work of farmers, grass-cutters, blacksmiths, butchers and so on. A lead singer may acclaim the skills or the efforts of individual workers, although these may not sing themselves. The custom of music-accompanied work is one of the many which died out in the slave plantation system.

Though examples of polyphony in African song are not as rare as they were once thought to be, they are rare enough in West Africa where the polyphonic songs of the Pygmies of the Ituri Forest with their delicate nuances or the many forms of polyphonic music among the Ghimira, Gidole or Aderi in Ethiopia, have no parallel. Generally speaking, West African collective song is anti-

Above: Hausa women grinding corn and singing competitive songs to the rhythm. One wears a 'mammy-cloth' printed with portraits of Queen Elizabeth the Second and Prince Philip.

phonal, following what has been frequently termed the 'leader-and-chorus' pattern. In this the vocal line of the leader is often improvised and changes with every verse sung, while the responses of the chorus vary little. A kind of harmony may result from the overlapping of lead line and chorus, but it is usually accepted, though not by Richard A. Waterman, that harmony is either not present, or is rudimentary. Choral singing is generally in unison or in organum, employing parallel octaves, parallel fifths, parallel fourths, thirds, or even in rare instances, parallel seconds. It has been pointed out by Father A. M. Jones that the tribes from Senegal to Nigeria – that is, in Negro rather than in Bantu Africa – sing in parallel thirds or in unison. Gunther Schuller has summarised that 'from this, one can assume that neither the unison nor the thirds group had much difficulty in integrating their melodies into Western harmony'. Unison singing was a practice in fundamentalist white churches while, as Schuller notes, 'the Western tradition between approximately 1700 and 1900 developed exclusively along the triadic principle of building harmonies in thirds'. Adaptation to Western custom in the Southern United States may have presented little basic difficulty to the slaves.

Where the difficulty may have arisen, it has been frequently suggested, was in the accommodation of African 'scales' with the Western diatonic. Ballanta Taylor posited an African scale of sixteen intervals in the octave; on the other hand many writers have assumed a pentatonic scale as being fundamental to African music. In jazz and blues the widespread use of 'blue notes', where the third and seventh degrees are flattened, has led to considerable speculation on the uncertainty of 'the African' in relating his concept of scale to the European diatonic. Though Father Jones has stated that he has 'never heard an African sing the third and seventh degrees of a major scale in tune' and has confirmed his impression that the so-called 'blue notes' are widespread among Africans, his observations were based on his knowledge of East and Central Africa – which probably contributed little to the slave trade. Other writers, including Alan P. Merriam and W. E. Ward, have concluded differently. 'In view of the evidence' wrote Merriam 'it seems safe to say that the "scale" of African music, if such exists, is diatonic in its major aspects, although exceptions occur and although there is certainly a considerable range of variation from area to area and even from tribe to tribe. The pentatonic is also widely used; the evidence for a sixteen-tone scale is scanty, indeed. Finally the question of the flattened third and seventh of the diatonic scale must be referred to future investigation.'

In his 'Cantometric' study of world *Folk Song Style and Culture* Alan Lomax has emphasised a 'remarkable homogeneity illustrated in the African map' and concludes that 'the Western Sudan clearly belongs with the Guinea Coast–Madagascar–Ethiopia–Northeast Bantu cluster. The Moslem Sudan lies between the two clusters.' His analysis of the regional profile in the cantometric chart states that it is 'dominated by the style features of the Bantu-African hunter core. The major approach to song is choral and antiphonal, with the characteristic use of overlap, so that at least two parts are frequently active at the same time. A well-blended, rhythmically tight, often polyphonic choral performance is the norm in most areas. The major vocal style is clear and unconstructed but with playful and intermittent use of high register, yodel, nasality, rasp and forcefulness. The melodic line is almost entirely free of ornamentation. Rhythm is strictly maintained. . . . Everything contributes to an open texture, inviting participation by a rock-steady beat, and by clear, liquid voices singing one note per syllable.' He concluded that 'the overall impact of the African style is multileveled, multiparted, highly integrated, multi-textured, gregarious, and playful-voiced.' This emphasis on choral song and relative disregard of the solo and duet forms invites argument. However, the 'Cantrometric Cultural Samples' for West Africa are themselves arguably grouped, the Western Sudan being represented by Malinke, Dogon and Diola-Fogny; the Guinea Coast by Baule, Fon, Toma, Susu-Mende, Yoruba, and inexplicably, Bambara; while Moslem Sudan consists of Hausa, Wolof and Fulani. Of all these only the Malinke, Yoruba and Hausa were chosen for Select Samples and Test Samples, and the Dogon and Toma were chosen for Select Samples only. On a world comparative basis this was no doubt all that was possible, but it is not altogether surprising that 'United States Negro' (unspecified) as a part of 'Afro-America' is included in the generalisation that the latter 'shows close similarities with the Guinea Coast and the Equitorial Bantu', hence the majority of American slaves were carried off by the slavers.' *Folk Song Style and Culture* therefore throws little light on the relationship of American Negro blues singing to the vocal forms of West Africa.

Such investigation may have to be undertaken further from the coastal regions, where, in Ashanti, for instance, Ward was basing his conclusions. In broad terms it would seem that the practice of embellishment and therefore very often of fluctuations and 'bends' in the notes becomes steadily more marked as one moves through the savannah regions to the desert. Perhaps it is the Arabic influence that determines this; or perhaps it is an outcome of the greater use of bowed string instruments which may both rival and stimulate the use of the voice. Certainly the ornamentation of the Tuaregs reaches a degree of enrichment that exceeds any in the blues and comes very close to that of *cante hondo* and *flamenco*. In the singing of many of the parkland and

Above: Tuareg woman playing the inzad. *Note the high bridge.*

semi-desert peoples the use of shadings and falling notes that approximate to those of the blues can be widely heard. Father Jones has spoken in general of 'the outline of an African tune' which he likens to 'a succession of the teeth of a rip-saw; a steep rise (not usually exceeding a fifth) followed by a gentle sloping down of the tune; then another sudden rise – then a gentle sloping down, and so on.' His description is broadly applicable to West African song and creates a picture of the falling sound of many vocal recordings. It does not, however, underline the calling character of much West African singing: the use of a high pitch, often an octave or two above the speaking voice of the singer, which is so marked a feature. I have continually had the impression in the singing of *griots* of the vocal line slipping back towards speech tones, to be hastily recalled to the high pitch with which the song started, before a slow downward drift begins once more.

To the element of pitch must be added that of attack. This seems to depend on whether the singer is directing his song to others, or whether he is singing mainly for himself. In the latter case the song is often soft and introspective, with an attention to melody which is 'musical' in the Western sense. As African song is often functional, and when not, is performed for the entertainment of others, it is frequently declamatory. The professional musician or entertainer who performs in the market place of a Hausa city, or who sings at feasts or at ceremonial functions in Mali or Upper Volta or Senegal, depends on the response of his audience. He may tell traditional stories in song, he may spread current news and gossip, he may taunt the unmarried men and raise laughs with *double-entendre* verses – but in the market place or beneath the shade tree he needs to be heard. With the high, projecting pitch he couples a strident, hard-edged vocal that cuts through the bustle and rumble of the market-place. Sometimes he will employ falsetto cries, sometimes he will sing a whole song in falsetto; shrieks and ululations are part of his vocal equipment. Deep chest tones from 'heavy' voices are extremely rare and seem to be reserved only for special rituals among certain tribes. In general, low voices with rich timbre and full, rounded tones are seldom used, while high, forced tones which drop to a speaking tenor are common.

How much of these elements in West African vocal tradition may be found in the blues? Though group singing is fundamental to both Negro church services and to the collective work songs that have persisted in the penitentiaries and penal farms of the Deep South, it is usual in the blues. On occasion blues musicians will sing together, even to the extent of sharing the same verses of a known and standard blues, but it is by no means common in the idiom. When it is to be heard, as in the recordings of some of the jug bands, it is almost invariably unison singing. Singing in parallel thirds would seem to be exceptionally rare in the blues, which is after all, as a vocal music, mainly performed solo. For this reason the antiphonal 'leader-and-chorus' patterns which have persisted so strongly in Negro religious song, and in the work songs, are unfamiliar in the blues vocal as such. But there is a frequently expressed opinion that the use of the 'answering' guitar in some blues traditions is a retention from the custom of leader-and-chorus singing. This would suggest, however, that the answering phrase should be standardised in each performance, as is customary in choral responses. It would seem more likely that if a retention from African practice is present, it is rather in the use of the stringed instruments by praise singers and others who use them imitatively to augment the content of their songs.

In vocal quality it would appear that the employment of high voices among certain blues singers – Sam Collins, Blind Lemon Jefferson, Barefoot Bill, Little Brother Montgomery, Kokomo Arnold among them – are closer to vocal practices in West Africa than are those like Charley Patton, Tommy McClennan or Blind Willie Johnson, who employed deep and sonorous voices or cultivated a deliberately low pitch. Though the rasp in the voice of a Bukka White can be compared with the strained tones of many African singers, its 'heaviness' cannot. Some blues singers use falsetto calls or may pitch part of a word an octave higher than the rest of the line: Tommy Johnson carried this technique to a refined degree. Others, like Arnold, may have used it with perhaps more spontaneity, though only an occasional blues singer appears to use his voice with the attack of the *griots*. Texturally there seem to be many points of correspondence and the deliberate rejection of qualities of European purity in blues singing would suggest a direct persistence of West African practice. Similarly the 'saw-tooth' pattern of the vocal is reflected in the blues, to be heard in the singing of artists as varied as Hambone Willie Newbern, Texas Alexander or Roosevelt Sykes. Alexander's voice, however, approximates to that of the soft-voiced African singers and does not have the strained and constricted character of the higher, tenser singers heard throughout the Sudan and reflected most dramatically in the singing of a Robert Johnson, or less intensely but consistently in the singing of a Frank Stokes. This soft-toned, introspective singing, representative of a whole tradition of African solo vocals, is mirrored in the recordings of Mississippi John Hurt, Furry Lewis, Peetie Wheatstraw, even Otis Spann. Embellishment of the vocal line is characteristic of blues and the use of sliding and passing notes is found in almost every blues singer's recordings. A Carl Martin or a Big Bill Broonzy extemporised with a greater freedom of inflection than many blues singers, but the use of elaborations was somewhat surprisingly developed more by the classic blues singers, and in particular Ma Rainey and Bessie Smith, than by the folk blues men.

The extent to which West African singers use expressive tone to extend the meaning of their words has not been ascertained, but it seems on aural evidence that vibrato, forced timbre and dropped notes are employed for dramatic effect. This is a blues

Above: Alex Moore sings with a soft burr, maintaining a vocal drone.

characteristic, although such techniques are more strikingly developed in Negro religious sermons by the so-called 'straining' preachers. In blues, expressive tone often means the dropping of the voice and the employment of gutterals, as in the singing of Bukka White: sometimes the vocal becomes more of a snarl. But gospel preachers frequently pitch up the voice when using this technique, dropping an octave at the ends of lines with a rough drone. Recordings of Bussani tribesmen in Upper Volta singing praise songs for the chief of the village of Yarkatenga reveal uncanny resemblances to the singing of straining preachers like Reverend Nix or Reverend Burnett. They also use a device much employed by Negro preachers, of cupping the left hand to the ear while singing with intense vehemence. Though blues singers are frequently also instrumentalists, those who only sing often employ the same technique: St Louis Jimmy for example and, it has been reported, Texas Alexander. The use of a drone or continuous humming between sung phrases is also a vocal feature shared by

Voltaic peoples and some blues singers such as Kokomo Arnold or Whistling Alex Moore.

Writing in 1899 on African survivals, Jeanette Robinson Murphy recalled that she had followed many 'old ex-slaves, who have passed away in their tasks, listened to their crooning in their cabins, in the fields, and especially in their meeting houses, and again and again they assured me the tunes they sang came from Africa'. Commenting on the inadequacies of transcriptions in the Jubilee and Hampton song books, she remarked that there was nothing to show the singer 'that he must make his voice exceedingly nasal and undulating, that around every prominent note he must place a variety of small notes, called "trimmings", and he must sing notes not found in our scale; that he must on no account leave one note until he has the next one well under control. He might be tempted . . . to take breath whenever he came to the end of a line or verse! But . . . he should carry over his breath from line to line and from verse to verse, even at the risk of bursting a blood vessel. He must often drop from a high note to a very low one, he must be very careful to divide many of his monosyllabic words in two syllables. . . . He must intersperse his singing with peculiar humming sounds – "hum-m-m".' To those accustomed to both blues and Sudanic singing these observations made halfway between the arrival of the last Africans on American shores and the present suggest some continuum of vocal traditions in delivery and conception.

Left: Arthur Crudup 'hollers' with a high-pitched voice. Right: a Bussani tribesman declaims like an Afro-American 'straining' preacher.

THE SOURCE OF THE SLAVES

If the evidence of their music suggests that the savannah peoples were the most influential in shaping the course of Afro-American music in the United States, what is the evidence of their presence among the slaves? Before any examination of the provenance of the slaves is made, in the first place it is necessary to consider how many slaves could in fact have brought any direct survivals from Africa with them. Over 300 years it has been estimated that anything between ten and thirty million African slaves were shipped from their homelands. J. C. Furnas estimates that between fifteen and twenty million arrived in the New World and that some three to four million died on the passage. 'The yearly average is something like 60,000 – less than one per cent of the total population of West Africa at any time up to 1800 . . .' With a population of Negro Americans which now exceeds twenty millions, it is somewhat surprising that in 1790 the total black population of the United States was only three-quarters of a million. Henry C. Carey's careful compilations show that the actual annual number of Negroes imported into North America averaged around 3,000 until 1760, rose to 7,400 in the following decade, fell to less than 2,000 a year for the next twenty years and rose again to nearly 4,000 up till the end of legal slavery in 1808. The total number imported and accounted for was 333,500; Gunnar Myrdal considered that 'a figure of slightly below 400,000 slaves imported before 1808 seems reasonable'. Even allowing for extensive smuggling of slaves after the abolition of slave trading, Myrdal concluded that 'whatever historical research ultimately determines these figures to be, it is extremely likely that the total number of slaves imported before 1860 by whatever means, was less than a million'. This means that authentic African 'survivals' can have been handed down only by extensive processes of enculturation, and that an acceleration of slave importation in the latter phases, legal or illegal, may have kept some of the memories fresh.

Perhaps the most thorough research on slave sources has been made by Melville Herskovits, who has shown the proportion of slaves brought from various sources and to various centres. Tabulating the materials kept in Virginia for the period 1710–1790, he noted that some 20,000 were given as 'Africa', 6,700 came from 'Guinea', 9,200 from Calabar (Nigeria), 3,800 from Angola and 3,600 from Gambia, including Senegal and Goree. His figures, quoting Miss Elizabeth Donnan for importations to South Carolina between 1733 and 1785, listed 18,000 from the Guinea Coast from Gold Coast to Calabar, some 22,000 from Angola and Congo and 16,500 from the Gambia to, and including, Sierra Leone. Though French ships going to the West Indies via Nantes showed a surprisingly low number of cargoes from Senegal, it is generally accepted that Senegal-Gambia, the Gold Coast and Calabar were the principal sources of African slaves for much of the trade, though Angola and Congo became sources of illegal trade through Portuguese trading. Arthur Ramos, in *The Negro in Brazil*, noted that 'at the beginning of the slave trade, the largest number of those imported into Brazil were from Angola, the Congo and Guinea. When more active communication began with Bahia, the leading source of supply was Guinea and the western Sudan. There began a remarkable influx of Yorubas, Minas from the Gold Coast, Dahomans and various Islamized tribes such as the Hausas, Tapahs, Mandingos and Fulahs.' Similarities between Negro music in the United States and that of Brazil have been noted and the possibility of common derivation demands more research.

For Herskovits the argument seemed proven that African survivals stemmed from what he termed the 'core area', the region of the Ashanti, Dahomey, Yoruba: the Akan, Fon, Ewe, and Twi speaking peoples of the Kwa group. All these fall within the greater, simpler subdivision of languages which distinguishes only the Sudanic, the Bantu and the Hamitic and forms a part of the Sudanic group. 'It is to be noted that the "typical" Sudanic forms of West Africa . . . Twi, Ewe, Fon, Yoruba – are the principal linguistic stocks of our "focal" area. This means that the slaves who came from them outside this focus spoke tongues related to those found at the center of slaving operations. Among the more important of these found in regions to the west of the "core" are the languages of the Gambia and Senegal (Wolof or Jolof), Sierra Leone (Temne and Mende), and the Middle Sudan (Mandingo). To the east are Ibo, Nupe, and Efik. To the north of the forested coastal belt Sudanic dialects also are spoken – Mossi, Jukun, and Kanuri among others.' Accepting that the

Map: Tribes of West Africa mentioned in the text. (Adapted from G. P. Murdock.)

Sudanic languages and cultures have much in common he stated, rightly enough, that 'in contrast to European custom, the resemblance of these coastal cultures to those of Senegal and the prairie belt lying north of the forested region of the west coast, or in the interior of the Congo, is appreciable.' In his view the 'core area', whose survivals are unquestioned in the West Indies as has been seen, dominated the others. 'It might be hazarded', he said with respect to the United States, 'that, in the instance of early Senegalese arrivals, whatever was retained of aboriginal custom was overshadowed by the traditions of the more numerous Guinea Coast Negroes; while as for late-comers such as the Congo Negroes, the slaves they found were numerous enough, and well enough established, to have translated their modes of behaviour – always in so far as Africanisms are concerned, and without reference to the degree of acculturation to European habits – into community patterns.'

In view of Melville Herskovits' detailed knowledge of Dahomey-Yoruba-Ashanti cultures and his familiarity with Negro cultures in Latin-America, this argument may be accepted for much of Central and South America. It was a guess 'hazarded' as far as the USA was concerned and merits questioning. Dr Lorenzo Turner's detailed studies of *Africanisms in the Gullah Dialect* showed that nearly 6,000 African words survived in the Sea Islands, representing nearly thirty West African languages. Among them are many examples of Fulah, Hausa, Mende, Mandingo,

Temne, Vai and other languages of the Senegal-Gambia, Sierra Leone and savannah peoples, as well as Twi, Yoruba and other survivals. Undoubtedly the high proportion of survivals from the coasts closest to the United States demands reconsideration of the problem. It has recently received attention from Professor David Dalby who notes that 'Senegambia, the nearest part of the Atlantic coast to North America, was a major source of slaves for the former English colonies, and many of these slaves were therefore conversant with the two main languages of Senegambia: Wolof and Mandingo'. The Wolof he notes 'were frequently employed as interpreters and mariners during early European voyages along the African coast. As a result the Wolof names of several African foodstuffs were taken into European languages, including 'banana' and 'yam'. It therefore seems reasonable to look for a possible Wolof influence on the development of American English vocabulary and the initial results of this investigation have been most encouraging.' Dr Dalby's extensive researches have revealed a remarkable incidence of Wolof survivals in terms and usages including a significantly high number in jazz usage: too high for mere coincidence. While he does not claim that all can be proven with certainty he does state that 'the frequency of these resemblances is unlikely to be the result of chance and points to the contribution of at least one African language to American vocabulary'. Researches in comparative studies with other African languages may make significant new discoveries.

The importance of the Senegambian slave trade lies in the accessibility of these ports to the Sudan savannah interior. Herskovits has contempt for what he terms the 'thousand-mile' theory, which argued that slaves were brought from deep in the interior. A trip of 1,000 miles was reported to have been undertaken by slaves on a number of occasions. Captain Samuel Gamble, for instance, was slaving off the coast of Sierra Leone in 1794 and reported that he saw about twelve vessels with a 'representation of a Lott of Fullows (i.e. Fulahs) bringing their slaves for a Sale to the Europeans which generally commences annually in December or early January, being prevented from coming down sooner by the river being overflow'd.' Gamble added that 'they sometimes come upwards of One Thousand Miles of the interior part of the country' and he noted that their 'Principal Places of trade are Gambia, Rio Nunez and the Mandingo country. Fifteen Hundred of them have been brought here in one Season. They are of (off) in May as the rains set in in June.' In exchange for the slaves he added 'their darling commodity that they get from the Whites is Salt'.

Only a year later Mungo Park arrived at Jillifree on the Gambia River and commenced his remarkable penetration of the Interior in search of the source of the Niger. His report of his exploration lends support to the argument that the music of the country was substantially the same in his day as it is now. He described the musical instruments of the Mandingoes, 'the principal of which are the *koonting*, a sort of guitar with three strings, the *korro*, a large harp with eighteen strings; the *simbing*, a small harp with seven strings; the *balafou*, an instrument composed of twenty pieces of hard wood of different lengths, with the shells of gourds hung underneath to increase the sound; the *tangtang*, a drum, open at the lower end; and lastly the *tabala*, a large drum commonly used to spread alarm throughout the country. Besides these, they make use of small flutes, bowstrings, elephants' teeth,

Below: these musicians depicted in Denham, Clapperton and Oudney's Narratives *were presumably* algaita *players from Western Sudan.*

and bells; and at all their dances and concerts, *clapping of hands* appears to constitute a necessary part of the chorus.'

Park's descriptions of the *korro* (kore) or *balafou* (baiafon) among others are clearly recognizable today. He also described the *griots*, or 'the *singing men*, called *Jilli kea*' who 'sing extempore songs in honour of their chief men, or any other persons who are willing to give "solid pudding for empty praise". But a nobler part of their office is to recite the historical events of their country; hence in war they accompany the soldiers to the field, in order, by reciting the great actions of their ancestors, to awaken in them a spirit of glorious emulation.' On his return, Park joined up with a slave coffle which was journeying to the coast from Kamalia. They were all prisoners of war who had been taken by the 'Bambarran army in the kingdoms of Wassela and Kaarta, and carried to Sego, where some of them had remained three years in irons'. From his descriptions of their movements it is evident that some had travelled 600 or 700 miles in fetters. They were joined by other groups of captives and a number of free persons, 'so that the number of free persons and domestic slaves amounted to thirty-eight, and the whole amount of the coffle was seventy-three. Among the free men were six Jilli keas (singing men), whose musical efforts were frequently exerted either to divert our fatigue, or obtain us a welcome from strangers.' The singing men marched in front of the coffle as they got beyond the limits of the Manding territory and when they arrived at a town retold in detail through their song the entire story of the travels of the coffle. When they finally arrived at Goree the total number of slaves prepared for shipment was 130. Because of the 'mode of confining and securing Negroes in the American slave ships' many of the captives suffered greatly; 'besides the three who died on the Gambia, and six or eight while we remained at Goree, eleven perished at sea, and many of the survivors were reduced to a very weak and emaciated condition.'

Though the numbers were not large compared with the great quantities of slaves shipped from the southern coast of West Africa, the numbers of slaves shipped from the Gambia in the 1730s was reaching as much as 2,000 a year and the competition between the French traders on the Senegal and the British on the Gambia kept a steady flow of slaves moving from the hinterland to the slave ships of Goree and St Louis. The Muslim penetration from the North meant that a great many scholars and Muslim missionaries with their personal slaves, as well as African traders

72

whose routes were often extended through vast tracts of country, were moving through the savannah regions. The unsettled nature of the country with the shifts of power occasioned by the wars of the Bambara, the Mandingos and the Fulani often meant that the travellers found themselves in hostile country subject to the attacks of raiding parties and ultimately themselves sold into slavery. This applied to Muslims from deep in the savannah and semi-desert regions who moved south, as well as to those who moved westwards. One who did was Abu Bakr.

Though he was born in Timbuktu in about 1790, Abu Bakr was raised in Jenne and completed his education in Bouna. Bouna is in the north-east of Ivory Coast and was then a centre for learned Muslims, their servants and slaves who had come from all over West Africa. The Ashanti warrior Adinkra attacked the town and after a severe battle, took it. 'On that very day they made me a captive. They tore off my clothes, bound me with ropes, gave me a heavy load to carry, and led me to the town of Bonduku, and from there to the town of Kumasi. From there through Akisuma and Ajumako in the land of the Fanti, to the town of Lago, near the salt sea (all the way on foot, and well loaded). There they sold me to the Christians, and I was bought by a certain captain of a ship at that time . . .' Abu Bakr was shipped to Jamaica, became the slave of a stonemason and there worked until he was freed, partially by public subscription in Kingston, in 1834. He was not a musician, he was not shipped to North America; his relevance here is only to demonstrate the routes and misfortunes that led a savannah Muslim into slavery and to being sold from the Guinea Coast, a sale made singular by his erudition, his scholarship, and his letters.

Mohammedans from the Savannah regions were certainly known on the plantations. Writing in *A Second Visit to the United States* in 1849, Sir Charles Lyell described life on the Hopeton plantation and the head driver, 'African Tom', a 'man of superior intelligence and higher cast of feature. He was the son of a prince of the Foulah tribe and was taken prisoner at the age of fourteen, near Timbuktou. The accounts he gave of what he remembered of the plants and geography of Africa . . . confirm many of the narratives of modern travellers. He has remained a strict Mahometan, but his numerous progeny of jet-black children and grandchildren, all of them marked by countenances of a more European cast than that of ordinary negroes, have exchanged the Koran for the Bible . . .' In 1901, Georgia Bryan Conrad recalled

Above: West Africa at the beginning of the nineteenth century. Though several locations are misplaced and ranges of mountains invented, the 'Yarraba', 'Ashantee', 'Bambarra', 'Feloops', 'Yaloofs' and other tribes are identified. Note also Biafra.

Negroes she had known forty years before: 'On Sapelo Island, near Darien, I used to know a family of Negroes who worshipped Mahomet. They were all tall and well-informed, with good features. They conversed with us in English, but in talking among themselves they used a foreign tongue that no one else could understand. The head of the tribe was a very old man called Bi-la-li. He always wore a cap that resembled a Turkish fez. These Negroes held themselves aloof from the others as if they were conscious of their own superiority.'

Salih Bilali, whose descendants were interviewed and discussed at length by Lydia Parrish in her *Slave Songs of the Georgia Sea Islands*, was born about 1770 near Mopti, some 700 miles from the coast in a Muslim Fulbe (Fulah) community. When he was about twelve years of age he was captured by Bambara slave raiders and taken to Segu 'and was transferred from master to master, until he reached the coast, at Anomabu. After leaving Bambara, to use his own expression, the people had no religion, until he came to this country.' In addition to his recollections noted by James Hamilton Couper and published in 1844, Salih Bilali wrote in Arabic a religious paper, long thought to be his 'diary'. Such Muslims, devout, learned and given positions of responsibility on the plantations, undoubtedly stood out from the rest. There is no reason to consider that the presence of Fulahs, Bambaras, Wolofs, Diolas, Hausas, Béri-Béri and other tribes from the savannah regions was rare in the plantations of the South. In his *Survey of the Supply, Employment and Control of Negro Labor*, Ulrich Bonnell Phillips specifically noted that 'in South Carolina, Negroes from Gambia, chiefly the Mandingoes, were the preferred ones, but those from Angola were quite acceptable'. While, to quote Gilberto Freyre, 'we also meet with references to Senegalese Negroes with their drop of Arabaic blood as being favoured for housework, by reason of their "greater intelligence".' The securing of slaves was done by the inhabitants of the mainland of Africa. 'The normal practice was for the Europeans to stay at the coast', noted Oliver and Fage. 'The earliest slaves to be exported were doubtless already slaves in their own communities, often criminals or debtors,' they wrote of the Guinea Coast, where 'invariably the Europeans bought their slaves from African kings and merchants'. Later, when the 'demand increased, peoples living just inland from the coast began to use the firearms they had acquired through trade to venture further into the interior and deliberately capture slaves for export.'

Though the Yoruba, Ibo, Fon and other tribes undoubtedly sent large numbers of their own tribesmen into slavery, the Ibo priests operating the 'Aro' system whereby witchcraft had to be paid for in captives, the consolidation of the coastal kingdoms, such as the federation of the Ashanti, strengthened them in their fight for more captives from the interior. 'The heart of the trade was the Slave Coast and the Gold Coast, and behind this territory extending into the interior for 700 miles or more. From this territory Senegalese Negroes, Mandingoes, Ibos, Efikes, Ibonis,

Karamantis, Wydas, Jolofs, Fulis, together with representatives of many of the interior Bantus were brought to 'America', recorded Weatherford and Johnson. This list includes many from the Guinea and Windward Coasts, but also those from far back into the savannah regions. Savannah tribes were in fact depopulated from both the west and the southern coast of the Guinea region: subjected to a pincer movement. Although on the coast the population may reach over a hundred persons to the square mile, only a short way back it rapidly diminishes and most of the savannah region and much of the rain forest has a population of less than twenty-five persons to the square mile. Such low population is due to many causes, but the authors of *Africa and the Islands* note that 'the slave trade certainly contributed to the sparseness of the population. Estimates of the volume of this trade vary, but it is possible that 20 million Negroes were exported to the Americas between the sixteenth and nineteenth centuries, and that many millions more were massacred in the process'. They added, moreover, that 'the trade in Negro slaves to the Islamic countries has been estimated at 10 to 15 millions. . . . The worst affected were the Sudanese Negroes and the Bantu'. Ignored by most writers on the subject were the interior wars caused by the spread of Islam, the rise of the Bornu states, the kingdoms of the Mande and the Bambara, and, at the very close of the legal slave trade, the rise of the Fulani empire which overthrew the Bornu and the Bambara states; these all provided captives and slaves for the markets of Timbuktu, Kano, or the traders from the coast. So it can be concluded that slaves were drawn not only from the 'true Negro' region of the Gold and Slave Coasts, Guinea and Calabar, but from deeper in the interior, and that these from the savannah regions, from the Senegambia and among the Wolof and Mandingo peoples, formed a not inconsiderable number of them. Their culture may have been transplanted to the United States in many forms, including that of music. It is even possible that they formed an unusually high proportion of the imported slaves. It has been established that slaves were sent often to the West Indies for acclimatisation before being distributed to various countries, including North America. It seems likely that those who coped best with the tropical heat and humidity and whose coastal rain forest environment was closest to that of the West Indies were kept in Latin America, while those who were accustomed to the Sudanese climate, with its somewhat more temperate but still extremely hot days, may have been chosen for shipment to the States. With them they may still have brought memories of their own traditions.

At this point it is instructive to return to the earliest reports of Congo Square (Congo Plains or Circus Square) in New Orleans. The architect Benjamin Henry Latrobe visited New Orleans in 1819 when the functions were at their height and there is little doubt as to the African survivals in the music and instruments described. Latrobe spoke of players of a cylindrical drum, of an open-staved drum and other drums of various kinds. He also described a 'most curious instrument' which was 'a stringed instrument which no doubt was imported from Africa. On the top of the fingerboard was the rude figure of a man in a sitting posture, and two pegs behind him to which strings were fastened. The body was a calabash.' Though there has been speculation on the origins of the instrument, Dr Curt Sachs suspecting a Congo origin, Lorenzo Turner pointed out that it could be found among the Hausa. The calabash bowl is of significance in a region of Louisiana where other materials were readily at hand, while the instrument has its parallels among some other savannah peoples. Writing in 1886, a lifetime later, George W. Cable described a scene of essentially similar character. Probably he was depicting events which he had seen earlier, for at one point he mentions slaves, and he had been in the city during and before the Civil War. Other estimates have suggested that he was depicting Congo Square in the 'eighties, but this is implicitly denied by Herbert Asbury who records that, in October 1817, the square 'was designated by the Mayor as the only place to which slaves might resort, and thereafter all such gatherings were held under police supervision. The dancing was stopped at sunset and the slaves sent home. Under these and other regulations the custom of permitting slave dancing in Congo Square continued for more than twenty years when it was abolished for reasons which the old city records do not make clear. It was resumed in 1845 . . . (and) reached the height of its popularity during the fifteen years which preceded the Civil War.'

According to Asbury the custom was abandoned in the troubled period following the Union occupation of New Orleans and would therefore have been concluded by the time Cable was writing. However, at that period, in the 'eighties, dances still continued in a vacant lot on Dumaine Street. Cable recalled the instruments he had seen with the accuracy of a close observer, at length and in great detail – drums, a gourd filled with pebbles, jews-harps, the jawbone of a mule or ox, empty casks and barrels. In his day, Negroes still played the 'Marimba brett, a union of reed and string principles. A single strand of wire ran lengthwise of a bit of wooden board, sometimes a shallow box of thin wood, some eight inches long by four or five in width, across which, under the wire, were several joints of reed about a quarter of an inch in diameter and of graduated lengths.' It was played by plucking the reeds with the thumbnails and was clearly the African *sansa* or thumb piano (and not, as the marimba name might suggest, a xylophone). 'But the grand instrument at last, the first violin, as one might say, was the banjo', he wrote. 'It had but four strings, not six: beware of the dictionary.'

An examination of his careful list of the tribes represented in Congo Plains is instructive. His principal descriptions were of those 'wilder than gypsies; wilder than the Moors and Arabs whose strong blood and features one sees at a glance in so many of them; gangs – as they were called – gangs and gangs of them, from this and that and yonder direction; tall, well-knit Senegalese from Cape Verde, black as ebony, with intelligent, kindly eyes and long, straight, shapely noses; Mandingoes, from the Gambia River, lighter of colour, of cruder form, and a cunning that shows in the countenance; whose enslavement seems specially a shame,

Left: a group of Savannah instruments including two sansas, *one made with cane tongues, the smaller with metal strips on a pilchard tin base. Also shown, a cane flute, a notched flute and a raft harp. Above: Napoleon Strickland plays a cane fife in Mississippi.*

their nation the merchants of Africa, dwelling in towns, industrious, thrifty, skilled in commerce and husbandry, and expert in the working of metals, even to silver and gold; and Foulahs, playful mis-called '*poulards*' – fat chickens – of goodly stature, and with perceptible rose tint in their cheeks; and Sosos, famous warriors, dextrous with the African targe: and in contrast to these, with small ears, thick eyebrows, bright eyes, flat upturned noses, shining skin, wide mouths and white teeth, the Negroes of Guinea, true and unmixed, from the Gold Coast, the Slave Coast and the Cape of Palms.' Later he described a dancer, a 'glistening black Hercules, who plants one foot forward, lifts his head and bare shining chest and rolls out the song from a mouth and throat like a cavern.' He had 'an African amulet that hangs about his neck – a *gree-gree*. He is of the Bambara, as you may know by his solemn visage and the long tattoo streaks running down from the temples to the neck, broadest in the middle, like knife gashes.' Even the name of the charm, a long established one in New Orleans rites, had similar ancestry, as Puckett noted:

'*grigri* (noun signifies "charm" – verb means "to bewitch") seem to be of African origin, the term *gris-gris* being employed in the Senegal as a general name for amulets.' But of all Cable's comments, one of the most telling occurs in his description of the *bamboula*, the celebrated dance of Place Congo and perennial attraction for visitors. 'The quick contagion is caught by a few in the crowd, who take up with spirited smitings of the bare sole upon the ground, and of open hand upon the thighs. From a spot near the musicians a single male voice, heavy and sonorous, rises in improvisation – the Mandingoes brought that art from Africa – and in a moment many others have joined in refrain, male voices in rolling, bellowing resonance, female responding in high, piercing unison.' Cable's description of the Bambara Negro in New Orleans is entirely in accord with Lafcadio Hearn's description in 1885 of 'The Last of the Voodoos', Jean Montanet. 'In the death of Jean Montanet, at the age of nearly a hundred years,

Vestigial voodoo: 'Essence of Fast Luck,' 'Sweet Mama Shake-Up' and High John the Conqueror root are still sold in the South.

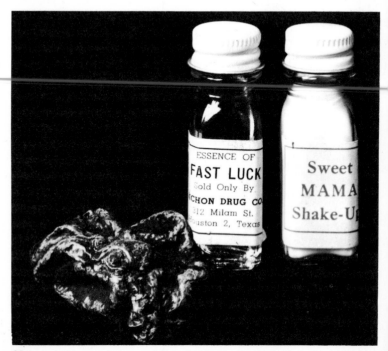

New Orleans lost, at the end of August, the most extraordinary African character that ever gained celebrity within her city limits', he wrote. 'He was a native of Senegal and claimed to have been a prince's son, in proof of which he was wont to call attention to a number of parallel scars on his cheek, extending in curves from the edge of either temple to the corners of his lips. This fact seems to me partly confirmatory of his statement, as Berengee Feraud dwells at some length on the fact that all Bambaras, who are probably the finest race in Senegal, all wear such configurations.'

Montanet was not the last of the Voodoos though he was among the last of his stature with a direct African background; Marie Leveau was born in New Orleans. With its flourishing cult of Voodoo, New Orleans was an exceptional American city, but it was exceptional, too, in permitting slaves such freedom of musical expression. Until the ordinance of 1817, slaves were permitted to congregate at weekends in many parts of the city for their dances and the dances in the confines of Congo Plains remained a major tourist attraction. Elsewhere, in the United States, slaves were not permitted to use drums. 'The slave-owners found to their cost that drums which beat for dances could also call to revolt, and thus it came about that in many parts of the New World, the African types of hollow-log drums were suppressed, being supplanted by other percussion devices less susceptible of carrying messages', wrote Herskovits. Though Courlander gives details of hollow log drums of comparatively recent date in the South, there was specific legislation in many states against the use of drums by Negroes, including the Black Codes of Georgia where 'beating the drum and blowing the trumpet' were forbidden, and Mississippi. A drum dated 1728 is displayed in the British Museum, made by a Negro in Virginia; but the use of the drums as a means of communication common to Ashanti, Yoruba and a number of other tribes might have led to slave revolts, and generally they were suppressed. The heavy restrictions imposed in all States following the Nat Turner insurrection of 1831 included forbidding Negroes to learn to read or write and also severe repression on music making which could incite slaves to violence or rebellion.

In 1803 New Orleans, as part of the Louisiana Purchase, became American. French traditions persisted and to some extent persist still, and among these was a liberalism towards the Negroes of the city not to be found elsewhere. The confining of

Above: hollow log drums, typical of the African rain forest, with pegged heads and 'dog-leg' angled drum-sticks.

slave celebrations to Congo Square might be seen as a contraction of those liberties, but drumming, along with other forms of musical expression, nevertheless continued in the predominantly Catholic city to a degree that the Protestant state could not tolerate. In New Orleans Negro smiths were engaged on work in wrought iron and the skills of the African blacksmith – who was frequently, as among the Bambara and Dogon, also the wood sculptor – were given rein. But, except in isolated instances on the Sea Islands and in Georgia graveyards, little of the African skills in the plastic arts survived in North America. The great traditions of wood carving, the masks and the ancestral figures which typified the arts of Ibo, Yoruba, Baule, Bambara, Dogon, Dan, Guere, Bobo or Mossi alike – both forest and savannah tribes – dissipated in the strict observances of Protestant America. Suppressed partly through godliness and partly through fear, they disappeared more completely than did even the drumming traditions. In Mississippi the drum-and-fife bands of Lonnie Young and Napoleon Strickland exist today as a possible African survival – though this is open to dispute: there is no hint of African plastic arts to be seen. To a great extent this reflects a difference of attitudes among Catholic and Protestant communities and, in James A. Porter's words, their influence 'in respect to cultural trends and Expression in the two American continents. While Catholic policy and practice seem deliberately to have encouraged and tolerated the African deviations from conventional Christian forms and then to have made it possible for the African bias to rise to the surface, Protestant dogma and cultural restrictions in the North utterly discouraged African religious traditions, extirpated them when they could be reached or by other repressive means prevented or nullified their influence. Nevertheless the abiding power of the African essence in Negro life is especially suggested in the folk creations of the North American Negro.'

Napoleon Strickland (cane fife) with his Como Band, including Other Turner (bass drum), and a snare drum of military type.

AFRICA AND
THE BLUES

'I made it out of a guitar neck and a tin pan my mama used to bake up biscuit-bread in. . . . If any of them livin' can remember back to the day of yesterday – it was a bread pan . . . but the old guitar, I bored a hole in the neck and run it through this here pan . . .' So Gus Cannon, or 'Banjo Joe', as he called himself, described his first instrument. Big Bill Broonzy told a similar story: 'When I was about ten years old I made a fiddle out of a cigar box, a guitar out of goods boxes for my buddy Louis Carter, and we would play for the white people's picnics . . .' The home-made instrument is almost a cliché of blues history and the description that Dave Mangurian made of Big Joe Williams' first guitar could be echoed in a score of interviews: 'When he was about six or seven years old he made a one-string guitar for himself by stapling two thread spools to a small box and stretching baling wire between the spools. He played it with the neck off a half-pint whisky bottle.' Many of these primitive instruments were monochords it seems. When I drew an illustration of Big Bill Broonzy as a boy, the singer commented 'man, that's just like me, like I was 'cept for one thing – my fiddle didn't have but one string on it.'

Many blues singers apparently first learned to play music on one-string instruments of their own manufacture. Children are the guardians of old traditions and customs and in the lore, language and games of children may be found clues to the history of centuries, and folk beliefs that may date to pagan origins. It does not seem unlikely that the custom of making a fiddle, guitar or banjo from available materials – lard can, broomhandle, fence picket, cigar box, or whatever may be at hand that meets the ingenuity of the maker – has a history that extends back to enslavement and beyond. Their counterparts in West Africa, meanwhile, make flutes out of bicycle pumps, sansas out of opened cans and monochords out of polish tins, such as I have collected for myself.

With the story of the first instrument runs another: the learning of the instrument from a relative, often the father or an uncle,

84

even a grandfather. Sometimes a visitor or neighbour in the community would be the principal influence. Rubin Lacy's story, as recounted by Dave Evans, may be considered fairly typical: 'His mother, half-brother and eldest brother were all good harmonica players . . . his brother-in-law, Walter McCray, was a good guitarist and singer of old songs like *John Henry* and *Stagolee* and *Rabbit on a Log*. Lacy didn't learn much from these people, however – although he liked their music. His real idol was George "Crow Jane" Hendrix. This man was a professional musician and the finest Lacy ever heard. He was old enough to be Lacy's father.' And Lacy himself stated: 'He could play anything he sat down to or anything he picked up, organ, piano, violin, bass, violin, mandolin, ukelele . . .' Rubin Lacy was born in 1901; Mance Lipscomb's memories go back a few years longer and his family associations extend back into slavery. As Mack McCormick reported: 'Mance's father was born a slave in Alabama. When still a boy he and his brother were separated from their parents

One- and two-stringed savannah instruments with hide or gut strings. The resonators are made from carved wood, a gourd and a Mansion Polish tin, the first two having goat-skin heads, sewn on when wet and allowed to tauten on drying.

and shipped to the newly settled Brazos bottoms of Texas. Then he made a fiddle out of a cigar box, and after emancipation became a full-time professional fiddler playing for dances in the Scotch-Irish, Bohemian and Negro settlements of the valley. . . . Mance was born on April 9, 1895 in Brazos County and when still a youngster he began travelling with his father, bassing for him on guitar.' He too, had musicians he admired, like Hamp Walker: 'About the best guitar man and songster as I ever met.'

Many of the older blues singers and songsters recall playing for white functions, and many of the veteran white musicians were impressed by their playing, as Tony Russell recounts in a parallel study. 'Now the first fiddle I ever heard in my life was when I was a kid,' recollected Hobart Smith, 'there was an old colored man who was raised up in slave times. His name was Jim Spenser . . . and he would come up to our house and he'd play one night for us, and he'd go on over to my uncle's house and play one night for them, and then go to my aunt's in the other hollow . . .' The techniques of playing their instruments were often picked up by the white musicians from the coloured ones. 'My younger brother Rosco brought a colored man home with him one evening who played with a brass band that used to be around Norton,' said the banjo player Dock Boggs. 'I heard him play *Alabama Negro*. He played with his forefinger and next finger – two fingers and thumb.'

A full documentation of the chain of influence and education whereby blues singers learned their instruments and their music would reveal much concerning the passing on of tradition and technique, while an impartial study of the people and places for whom they played might be instructive on the meeting of black and white music. It is clear from present knowledge that the processes of acculturation and enculturation are both present in Negro music as we know it, with much of the blues containing elements that come essentially from the European dance and ballad traditions, and yet having a character that is distinct and special.

It seems possible that some of the distinctive elements have a history that extends far back into slavery and that they have within them, as this book has attempted to show, some features which may well be inherited from West Africa. But, it is my contention, not from the 'West Africa' that has been assumed in most writings on jazz and related subjects. To summarise, it seems to me that the whole conception of music in the rain forest regions, and especially in the drum orchestras, has little to do with the folk music of the American Negro, whatever it may have had to do with jazz. The evidence of the music of the Ashanti, Yoruba, Ewe and Baule is of music of great rhythmic complexity which seems not to have survived in any significant way in the United States. That it is to be heard in a remarkably pure form in Haiti and other parts of the West Indies serves to emphasise that, given the right hospitable circumstances, this powerful music can thrive on foreign soil after the passing of a century and much more. But, like other aspects of rain forest culture and the image-making of African sculpture, when it ran counter to the patterns of behaviour acceptable to the American slave-owners, it died.

In contrast to the music of the drum-dominated tribes of the coastal regions, the music of the savannah Sudanic regions appears to have been of a kind that would have accorded well with the Scots and English folk forms and been acceptable enough to have survived among the slaves. The banjo, as we have seen, survived and flourished, while the skills of the players of *kukuma* or *goge*

Zachary, Louisiana. James 'Butch' Cage plays fiddle, Willie Thomas plays guitar and his wife 'pats Juba' in rhythm.

would soon have been adapted to the European fiddle under active encouragement. And encouragement was certainly there, as 'A small Farmer' wrote in *De Bow's Review*, acknowledging that 'Negroes are gregarious; they dread solitariness, and to be deprived from their little weekly dances and chit-chat . . . I have a fiddle in my quarters, and though some of my good old brethren in the church would think hard of me, yet I allow dancing; ay, I buy the fiddle and encourage it, by giving the boys occasionally a big supper.' Another slave-holder, describing the management of his plantation in the same periodical, remarked that he 'must not omit to mention that I have a good fiddler, and keep him well supplied with catgut, and I make it his duty to play for the Negroes every Saturday night until 12 o'clock. They are exceedingly punctual in their attendance at the ball, while Charley's fiddle is always accompanied with Ihurod on the triangle, and Sam to "pat".' As one old slave, Cato, who was born in 1836 near Pineapple in Alabama, remarked: 'We used to have frolics, too. Some niggers had fiddles and played the reels and niggers love to dance and sing and eat.'

Under these circumstances the musicians among the slaves from Senegal, Gambia, Mali, Upper Volta, Niger, Northern Nigeria and other savannah regions corresponding to the territories within these present political boundaries, found opportunities to profit from their skills. Negro musicians were encouraged to play for plantation dances and balls at the 'Big House' and exercising their abilities gave them a chance to escape the drudgery of field work. The bands of fiddles, banjos, tambourines and triangles accompanied by slaves 'patting Juba' on thighs and knees, meant that Bambara and Wolof, Mandingo and Hausa had the opportunity to play in groups of a kind to which they were accustomed, and on instruments with which they were more or less familiar. It seems likely that the guess which Melville Herskovits hazarded to the effect that 'in the instance of the early Senegalese arrivals, whatever was retained of aboriginal custom was overshadowed by the traditions of the more numerous Guinea Coast Negroes' may well have been very wide of the mark. On the contrary, they may have found themselves considerably at an advantage in a community where the playing of drums was largely discouraged. Notwithstanding their numerical inferiority, they may have established themselves very well as musicians. In fact the rider that Herskovits made, that late-comers found the earlier Negroes 'well enough established to have translated their modes of behaviour . . . into community patterns' could well operate against his argument. The slaves from the Senegambia were early on the scene and by this token had the longest opportunity to establish their role within the community pattern.

Though there is considerable evidence to support this hypothesis, it is readily acknowledged that there is too little available data for conclusive argument. To a large extent the documentary and other source material could well be examined again without the conditioning and limiting assumption that the majority of the slaves came from the rain forest tribes. Careful scrutiny of the surviving records of plantations might reveal clues as to the provenance of many of the slaves, which a thorough knowledge of the distribution of tribes throughout West Africa and not merely in the coastal regions may make more significant. The logs of slavers' ships and the books of the slave-traders may merit re-examination, while the records of the import of slaves to the West Indies and subsequent export to the United States could be informative. Slaves who were most able to cope with malarial infection, with tropical heat and high humidity may have been kept back for work in the West Indies plantations, while those who came from the regions beyond the rain forest and who were accustomed to conditions somewhat closer to those of North America may have been shipped there later.

It seems possible then, that work along the lines of Elizabeth Donnan's monumental *Documents Illustrative of the Slave Trade to America* and other sources, with a more careful consideration of the map of West Africa, may reveal patterns of importation. Records of the export of slaves from the coastal ports might also be revealing; it seems inadequate to assume because slaves were shipped from the Gold and Slave Coast forts, that they were therefore members of the rain forest tribes. As has been seen, there is evidence to suggest that a great many came from the interior, deep in the Sudan, having been passed from trader to town on a southbound route that would culminate at the shipping ports. Bearing in mind, however, that few of the shippers and traders were greatly concerned with the origin of their slaves, except perhaps for meeting the special preferences of buyers, a large resource of information cannot be anticipated. But we might turn with profit to the developing sciences in the study of race.

Mention has already been made of sickle cell distribution in West Africa. Sickle cell distribution is closely related to the prevalence of malarial-bearing mosquitos, but as Frank B. Livingstone has shown in a detailed analysis of the implications of the sickle cell gene distribution in West Africa, it has been greatly conditioned by patterns of subsistence economy and the movement of peoples and tribes. The results can be confusing for 'in many cases there are significant differences in the frequency of the trait even within the same tribe. For example, the Fulani have frequencies ranging from 8 to 25 percent, and the Mandingo in the Gambia vary from 6 to 28 percent. Although this great variability impedes analysis about the distribution, some significant generalizations can nevertheless be made. Broadly speaking, the higher frequencies tend to be toward the south, and despite many exceptions, there is some indication of a north-south gradient in the frequency of the sickle cell trait.' Perhaps this is too little to go on, but the distribution map shows a wide Sudanic belt where the distribution is less than eight percent, while the Kwa-speaking peoples – Ewe, Fanti, Twi, Ashanti, Yoruba among them, have readings higher than twenty percent. It is interesting to note that the inhabitants of Liberia, which was largely settled by repatriated slaves, offers readings from nil to only two percent. This might imply that the genetic decline had resulted from the importation of slaves with relatively low counts to North America, where malarial infestation was too low to promote further distribution of the sickle cell gene. Though such genetic analyses among Negroes, and blues singers in particularly, would be of great interest, it is highly unlikely that the research will ever be undertaken.

Nevertheless, analyses of gene flow from the white population to the Negro population in America have been made. Dr Bentley Glass and Dr C. C. Li used samples from South African Bantu, East Africans and Egyptian Sudanese for their studies and these have been questioned by D. F. Roberts who noted that 'the extensive researches of Herskovits showed that the provenance of the Negro slaves in the USA was of more limited area than had been earlier thought. A few were derived from Madagascar and east coast localities, but the large majority originated from the western regions of Africa.' In his re-analysis Roberts unfortunately took Herskovits' writings literally and without the re-examination of these assumptions, which he applied to his own field. Thus his African samples were drawn from the Ewe, Ashanti, Yoruba, S.E. Nigeria (presumably Ibo) and the only examples from savannah regions were in northern Nigeria and the Jos Plateau. This meant that Mande-speaking peoples were entirely omitted from his samples. The American Negro samples from which the calculations of gene flow were deduced were drawn almost entirely from Baltimore, Washington and New York with an isolated 'Southern' instance (Ohio). Again, gene-flow analyses which drew samples through other regions of West Africa and from Negroes in the Deep South might be revealing in their results.

Such studies reflect Herskovits' own analyses of 'racial crossing', first published in *The American Negro* in 1928. In his anthropometric comparisons of Africans he used the available data on samples taken among the Ekoi (south-east Nigeria), but also from among the Vai from the Ivory Coast and the Kagoro, a scattered tribe living among the Bambara and Soninke. The small samples – ranging from a score from one tribe to seventy in another – were commented on at the time, and raised some doubt as to the validity of the comparisons with nearly 1,000 'mixed American Negroes'. Of his American samples nearly 500 were from Howard University, more than 200 from Harlem and less than a hundred from 'West Virginia rural'. Again, the African samples were probably not widely enough distributed to be significant, while the predominance of northern Negroes and those from the social upper class, against virtually no representation of statistics from the Deep South, probably strongly affected his conclusions as to the emergence of an American Negro type. To the observer without the benefit of statistical analysis the physical types represented among blues singers are by no means always typically West African rain forest, and neither are they consistent within the group. There is little relationship to one type, American Negro or otherwise in say, Leroy Carr, Roosevelt Sykes, Big Joe Williams or Clifton Chenier. On the other hand, some singers, like Big Bill Broonzy, Little Son Jackson, John Lee Hooker, or Sunnyland Slim have features which could merge easily enough among the Ashanti or the Yoruba. Most striking to me, however, is the predominance of certain physical characteristics among a large number of blues singers which relate closely to those of savannah peoples. The high cheek-bones, long features, narrow jaw-lines and, frequently, straight noses, of a surprisingly large number of blues singers has been previously unremarked, although applicable to many of them. In such singers as Fred McDowell, Scott Dunbar, Carl Martin, Bumble Bee Slim, Sleepy John Estes, Honeyboy Edwards, Tommy and Mager Johnson among many

The facial features of the late John Henry Barbee from Tennessee and Aaron 'T-Bone' Walker from Texas, would not appear out of place in the Savannah regions of West Africa.

others, these characteristics are markedly present. In some cases the straight nose becomes even hooked, as in the case of Yank Rachell; in others the long features are particularly pronounced, as with Doctor Ross; in still others lean features are deeply outlined from the sides of the nose to the chin as in the cases of T-Bone Walker or Elmore James. 'The typical Mandingo,' wrote C. G. Seligman, 'are described as tall and slender in build, with finer features, fuller beard, and lighter skin that the neighbouring populations.' Of the Songhai he wrote that physically they 'are moderately tall, with a stature of about 68 inches. They are long-headed, with a cephalic index of 75.5, their northern blood being especially obvious in their relatively well-formed noses. . . . Other evidence is to be found in their skin colour, which is described as coppery-brown, never of the dark, almost black colour of the Negroes of Dahomey and Ghana. Their hair, however, is always spiralled.' Such descriptions could well apply to a large number of blues singers, whose presence in the regions stretching east from Senegal for 1,500 miles would not be physically out of

92

place. It may be noted that many of the peoples who come within this belt *are* very dark, the Wolof being among the blackest of all African peoples, although refined and well-made in feature and build.

Of course, such comparisons are subjective and unscientific, but they are striking enough nevertheless. It could be argued that the influence of inter-breeding with North American Indians – several blues singers claiming such ancestry – might account for the physical features mentioned above. While recognising that such claims are made by many Negroes and a high proportion of Herskovits' and Meier's subjects, Dr Bentley Glass, in a paper 'on the Unlikelihood of Significant Admixture of Genes from the North American Indians in the Present Composition of the Negroes of the United States' has brought careful evidence to refute this argument in general, if not in the case of blues singers in particular. In cases where miscegenation has clearly accounted for marked Caucasian features, as in the instances of Charley Patton, or the Chatman family, it is not suggested that any inherited physical characteristics might be savannah in origin.

Another area which might merit further study is that of linguistic analysis. If the music of the 'shout' (from, as noted above, the Bambara *saut*) has traceable savannah associations, what of the music of the jukes? Dr Lorenzo Turner has traced the very word *juke* to the Gullah *joog*, meaning in the Georgia Sea Islands, 'disorderly'. This in turn he has traced to the original Bambara *dzugu* meaning 'wicked'. Dr David Dalby has drawn some remarkable comparisons between Wolof words and currently surviving American Negro usage, relating 'jive' talk to the Wolof *jev*, meaning 'to talk disparagingly'; 'hip' to the Wolof *hipi*, meaning 'to open one's eyes'; and the jazz term to 'jam' to the Wolof word *jaam* for slave. Does the name of one of the more primitive savannah tribes – the Bobo – remain in the title and words of the dance-song *Georgia Bobo*, or *Louisiana Bobo* and the line from the *Dozens*: 'if you ain't doin' the bobo, what's your head doing down there?' Perhaps the frequent use of a number of words in the blues which appear in no American lexicon may eventually be traced back to such origins.

Whatever the outcome of anthropological research might be, whether in the analysis of genetic flow or anthropometric statistics (and one must admit that the chances of any such analysis being made among blues singers is, to say the least, slim); whatever historical or linguistic research may uncover; ultimately the most important area of examination must be that of musical analysis. This may well mean the upsetting of old theories concerning the relation of jazz and blues. As Charles Duvelle, writing on the music of Upper Volta, has observed: 'The usual hypothesis is that Negroes of African origin used to sing on a pentatonic scale and that when they attempted to sing Lutheran hymns, based on a heptatonic scale, they had to deform the 3rds and 7ths, which

were unknown to them, these alterations leading to the "blue notes" characteristic of jazz music. But this theory is ill-founded in assuming that the pentatonic scale was the only one used by the Negroes, while in fact there is sufficient evidence that other scales were used in Africa, including the heptatonic. Moreover, the "blue notes" themselves are found in Africa. Many other features of jazz music (its formal rhythmic and polyphonic characteristics) are also found in Africa.' Tolia Nikiprowetzky in fact has noted that in Senegal 'nearly all pieces are based on heptatonic scales, which could be compared to a nontempered variety of modal scales'.

Musicological analyses of the blues have scarcely been undertaken to date and John Fahey's study of the structure of Charley Patton's repertoire, which it is hoped will be published in this series, is singular. Future studies which examine the scales and structures in the blues would make a basis for comparison with those employed in the savannah regions of West Africa. Similarly the melodic lines employed by the *griots* could be examined against those of the blues singers, and with appropriate equipment (such as Metfessel's phonophotography), the employment of

A comparison between the finger positions of the Senegal griot *Aamadou Coly Sall (left) and those of banjo player Beauford Clay and guitarist Blind James Campbell (right) of the Nashville String Band suggests related playing techniques.*

95

evidence to show that this is by no means a new phenomenon in the blues; the triggered responses that B. B. King may invoke with the first few notes of his guitar seem to be of a similar kind to those produced by Tommy Johnson as he swung into his particular rhythm pattern. Again, if songs of praise are not now a strong feature of the blues, the blues singer's predecessors sang of traditional heroes in *John Henry*, the *Boll Weevil* and other ballad subjects which clearly emphasised values. Songs of ridicule on the other hand, persist still, with the *Dirty Dozen* having a long history. Until a couple of decades ago the blues still commented liberally on current events with disasters and participation in the Second World War being recorded fairly frequently. At a subtle level the blues also operated as a vehicle for social control, with the attitudes of the black society fairly represented within the songs. Admired characteristics, especially physical ones, have also been prominent in the blues and attitudes of mind and aspects of personal behaviour are frequently criticised. With the demise of the work song, the blues became the song vehicle to accompany labour and, in earlier years, for the medicine show or the barber shop; and, most obviously and persistently, for restaurants and bars, the blues has been used to attract custom. Mass media have made this role effective on a larger scale, for blues still drums custom for baking flour or a multitude of consumer goods on radio. Only in the field of political activity does the blues seem to have remained neutral in comparison with the functions Ames describes.

There seem to be many interesting parallels between the attitudes of the savannah communities to the *griot* and those of the black community to the blues singer which also bear comparison. Blues singers are not necessarily socially acceptable in the black community, but they are certainly known to most members of it. They, too, are the source of humour and entertainment, of gossip and comment, and a singer like Lightnin' Hopkins is very much a *griot* in personality, with a similar flair for spontaneous and devastating comment on the passing scene. But if blues singers appeal because of these talents as well as their musicianship, they are, like the *griots*, frequently considered as lazy, lacking in industry and job application. In similar fashion many blues singers hire themselves to a single employer or are closely affiliated for long periods with one patron, club or bar; but there are like-

Counterparts of the griots *in Maxwell Street market, Chicago.*

Above: Texas Blues singers Manny Nichols (guitar) and O. Z. Steen (fiddle) have a comparable place in their society to that of such griots as Sosira and Kunaal (right) among the Grunshi peoples of Northern Ghana and Upper Volta.

wise blues singers who are free agents and who, like Big Joe Williams, say, are continually on the move, obtaining employment where and for as long as they wish. Not a few blues singers make – and sometimes lose – considerable sums of money through their work, especially those like Muddy Waters or Howling Wolf who have a record company as patron. These singers work with groups today, rather than as solo singers. Like the *griot*, there are individual performers, duos and small groups, similarly depending on stringed instruments, the occasional horn, and rhythmic accompaniment. Those qualities of light rhythm, swing and subtle syncopation which characterise the music of many blues singers, those aptitudes for improvisation in music and in verse, those repertoires of traditional songs, stock-in-trade lines and phrases and sudden original words and verses – all these are no less recognisably the hallmarks of the *griots*.

Further examination might uncover in detail close correspondences in content and approach: there is in blues a sizeable body of fairly obscene song, little recorded in unexpurgated form, but familiar in euphemism and *double-entendre*; this too is familiar among the *griots*, but recordings and text analyses are still woefully few. To what extent any similarities are coincidental and arising from parallel situations would also have to be examined, and a detailed study of the growth of Negro singers and groups in the slave period in North America might be revealing on this aspect also. For all this is largely speculative, even if the speculations are based on a considerable body of material which has been little related in the past. As this study is concerned with the possibility of African retentions in the blues, and a consideration of where, in 'Africa', these traditions may have originated, little has been said of jazz. As blues is sung and played mainly on string instruments and the piano, with harmonicas, kazoos, and occasional rhythm and wind instruments augmenting, the prevalence of the counterparts of some of these instruments in the savannah regions has been emphasised. Jazz, however, is a music of wind instruments against rhythm sections. Hardly any mention has been made here of the *griot* orchestras of drums and horns, or of drums alone, which may also be found in the savannah. But it has been shown that the techniques of complex rhythms, of 'speaking' instruments and vocalisation are not peculiar to the drum orchestras of the rain forest, but are shared by the musicians and groups of the savannah belt. It may be found necessary in the future to write a new chapter in the history of the blues, which examines the extent and the source of African retentions in the music. But it may also be necessary to re-write the first chapter in every history of jazz.

NOTES

Chapter 1. Africa and the Jazz Historian

Melville Herskovits published *The Anthropometry of the American Negro* in 1930 (Columbia University Press). His quoted conclusions appear on p. 177. In *An American Dilemma* (Harper & Row edition, 1962) Gunnar Myrdal's team analyse this and other data in Chapter V. Professor von Hornbostel's propositions were questioned by Herskovits in 'The Negro in the New World', an article in *American Anthropologist*, vol. 32, no. 1, 1930, pp. 146–7. Herskovits also discussed in *Cultural Anthropology* (Alfred A. Knopf, 1955) the subjects of acculturation, pp. 471–9, and enculturation pp. 327–32 and 453–4.

Shining Trumpets by Rudi Blesh (Cassell, 1949) examines African music and its relation to jazz on pp. 25–46. So does Marshall Stearns in *The Story of Jazz* (Sidgwick & Jackson, 1957) pp. 3–64. Similar space is devoted to the subject in Gunther Schuller's *Early Jazz* (Oxford University Press, 1968) pp. 3–62. Other views are expressed in *Jazz Hot and Hybrid*, Winthrop Sargeant (Dutton, 1946) pp. 149–57, 220; Robert Goffin's *Jazz – From the Congo to the Metropolitan* (Doubleday, 1946) pp. 7–30; Leonard Feather's *The Book of Jazz* (Arthur Barker, 1957) pp. 10–12; and Francis Newton's *The Jazz Scene* (MacGibbon & Kee, 1959) pp. 39–40. The quotation from André Hodeir comes from his *Jazz: Its Evolution and Essence* (Grove Press, 1956) p. 42.

The references to Ernest Borneman's writings include his articles 'Creole Echoes' in *Jazz Review* for September and November 1959 and 'The Roots of Jazz' in *Jazz, New Perspectives*, ed. Hentoff and McCarthy (Rinehart, 1959). His booklet *An Anthropologist Looks at Jazz* was published by Jazz Music Books, 1946, and the quotations appeared on pages 9 and 10. Harold Courlander's *Negro Folk Music U.S.A.* (Columbia University Press, 1963) discusses 'Blues' in Chapter VI and lays great emphasis on African survivals in American Negro music. Richard Alan Waterman's important paper on 'African Influence on the Music of the Americas' appeared in *Acculturation in the Americas* (Sol Tax, ed.) (University of Chicago Press, 1952) pp. 207–18.

Herskovits' 'Scale of Intensity of New World Africanisms' illustrated his paper 'Problem, Method and Theory in Afroamerican Studies' in *Afroamerica*, I, 1945, pp. 5–24 and the quotation from *New Republic*, vol. 84, no. 1083, published in 1935 comes from an article on 'What Has Africa Given America?' pp. 92–4. Herskovits published his extensive findings on African survivals in the Americas in his invaluable if controversial *The Myth of the Negro Past* (Beacon reprint, 1958); see particularly for West Indian survivals, pp. 246–7.

William Russell's comments appear in a letter to the author for July 1968 and the extensive study of early fiddles and fifes appears in Henry A. Kmen's *Music in New Orleans – The Formative Years 1791 – 1841*, from Chapter XII of which, 'Negro Music', come most of the references here, except the quotation from George Washington Cable's celebrated article 'The Dance in the Place Congo', originally published in *Century* magazine for February 1886 and reprinted in *Creoles and Cajuns*, ed. Arlin Turner (Doubleday Anchor, 1959). Thomas Jefferson's oft-quoted note on the *banjar* appears on p. 19 of his *Notes on Virginia*, and early minstrelsy is discussed in *Gentlemen, Be Seated* by Sigmund Spaeth and Dailey Paskman (Doubleday Doran, 1928) pp. 11–19. The quotation from Fanny Kemble comes from her *Journal of a Residence on a Georgia Plantation 1838–1839* (Alfred A. Knopf, 1961), p. 131. In *The Peculiar Institution* (Random House, 1946), pp. 367–70, Kenneth Stamp gives references on Negro music. *The Bluesmen* by Samuel B. Charters, is published by Oak Publications (1967), and the references to African influence on blues are on pp. 16–20. *The Musical Instruments of the Native Races of South Africa*, by Percival R. Kirby (Witwatersrand, 1934), discusses and illustrates the ramkie and associated instruments. See also *Musical Instruments. A Comprehensive Dictionary*, by Sibyl Marcuse (Doubleday & Company, 1964).

Chapter 2. Music in West Africa

The fullest discussion of the roles of music in Ashanti society appears in the descriptions of ritual in *Religion and Art in Ashanti*, by R. S. Rattray (Oxford University Press, 1927), while the roles and kinds of drums are detailed in *Drumming in Akan Communities of Ghana*, by J. H. Kwabena Nketia (University of Ghana, 1963). Alan P. Merriam's classification of musical regions in Africa appears in his study 'African Music' in *Continuity and Change in African Cultures*, ed. William R. Bascom and Melville Herskovits (University of Chicago Press), pp. 76–80. See 'African Influence' above for Waterman's concept of 'hot' rhythm.

Olaudah Equiano's autobiography, published as *The Interesting Narrative of Olaudah Equiano, or Gustavus Vass, the African* was first published in London in 1789; the quotation comes from Chapter I. The discussion of Yoruba drums appears in Anthony King's *Yoruba Sacred Music* (University of Ibadan Press, 1961), in the Introduction. A. M. Jones' *Studies in African Music* is published by Oxford University Press, 1959, and his paper on 'African Rhythm' was published in *Africa*, vol. 24, no. 1, January 1954; the quotation comes from p. 39. J. H. Kwabena Nketia's paper on the *History and Organisation of Music in West Africa* is published by the University of Ghana, c. 1959. Other references are from his *Drumming in Akan Communities* (above) p. 166 and pp. 22–3, and his paper *Historical Evidence in Ga Religious Music* [Institute of African Studies (Ghana), 1962]. Harold Courlander's comments on the African drum in North America appear in his notes to *African and Afro-American Drums* (Folkways Record Album no. FE4502 C/D). Other references to Waterman and A. M. Jones come from sources already cited.

Joseph H. Greenberg's *Studies in African Linguistic Classification* (Compass Publishing Co., New Haven, 1955) is the standard work on this subject, but he also contributes an article on 'Africa as a Linguistic Area' in Bascom and Herskovits' *Continuity and Change* (above). For African climate and topography see, for instance, *Africa and the Islands* by Church, Clarke, Clarke P. J. H., and Henderson (Longmans, 1964) and *Africa: Regional Economic Atlas*, P. H. Ady (Clarendon Press, Oxford, 1965). For tribal distribution see *Africa: Its Peoples and their Culture History*, G. P. Murdock (McGraw-Hill, 1959).

For details of the *griots* the notes to *Niger, la Musique des Griots* (Disques Ocora OCR20), and

La Musique Des Griots (Disques Ocors, OCR15) by Tolia Nikiprowetsky, who made the recordings, are exemplary. Other comments come from Curt Sacha, *The Wellsprings of Music*, ed. Jaap Kunst (McGraw-Hill, 1965), p. 205, and William Seabrook in *Jungle Ways* (Harrap, 1931) pp. 35–8. The notes on the *griots* among the Dan are by Hugo Zemp for *The Music of the Dan* (UNESCO Collection BM30L2301) and *The Music of the Senufo* (UNESCO BM30L2308). The *gewel* are described by David Ames in the notes to *Wolof Music of the Senegal and the Gambia* on Folkways FE4462, where he compares the *halam* to the banjo. David Ames also made the recordings and wrote the notes for *Nigeria-Hausa Music*, Volumes 1 and 2 (UNESCO BML2306 and 2307). All these recordings are recommended to those who wish to study musical examples of the *griots* and professional Savannah musicians.

Chapter 3. Savannah Song
William Smith's *A New Voyage to Guinea* (1745) is quoted in Douglas Grant's *The Fortunate Slave: An Illustration of Slavery in the Early Eighteenth Century* (Oxford University Press, 1968) p. 10, and Mungo Parks' *Travels in Africa* (1798) has been reprinted by Dent's 'Everyman's Library', 1969. See p. 30.

For a mid-'thirties description of a 'ring-shout' see Chapter III of Carl Carmer's *Stars Fell on Alabama* (Lovat Dickson, 1935). Lydia Parrish discusses ring-shouts at length in Chapter III of *Slave Songs of the Georgia Sea Islands* (1942) (Folklore Associates, 1965) and quotes Dr Lorenzo Turner on the subject. Work songs of the Senegal Casamance are discussed in the notes to his recordings of *The Music of the Diola-Fogny of the Casamance, Senegal*, by J. David Sapir (Folkways FE4323). African song is discussed (pp. 91–5) in *Folk Song Style and Culture*, by Alan Lomax (American Association for the Advancement of Science, 1968). The list of tribes selected for the cultural sample is on pp. 32–3.

Quotations and references to the writings of Father Jones, Gunther Schuller and Alan P. Merriam are as given in the notes to Chapter II above. The singing styles of the Boussani and tribes from Upper Volta are discussed in the notes to his recordings, by Charles Duvelle, in *Haute Volta* (Disques Ocora SOR10). Jeanette Robinson Murphy's article from *Popular Science Monthly*, 1899, on 'The Survival of African Music in America' is reprinted in *The Negro and His Folk-Lore*, ed. Bruce Jackson (University of Texas Press, 1967), pp. 331–2.

Chapter 4. The Sources of the Slaves
For J. C. Furnas' analysis of the numbers of slaves imported to North America see his *The Road to Harper's Ferry* (Faber and Faber, 1961), pp. 111–2. Henry C. Carey's figures appear in Gunnar Myrdal's *An American Dilemma* (as above) p. 118. The sources of the slaves as published by Melville Herskovits appear in *Myth of the Negro Past*, pp. 46–53, and his arguments as to the linguistic stocks and the 'core area' appear on pp. 79 and 295. Arthur Ramos' *The Negro in Brazil* translated by Richard Pattee (Washington, 1939) gives details of the sources of slaves to South America. See also, for comparison, Gilberto Freyre, *The Masters and the Slaves* (Alfred A. Knopf, 1946).

Dr Lorenzo Turner's *Africanisms in the Gullah Dialect* (University of Chicago Press, 1949) gives extensive African survivals in speech and Dr David Dalby's comparison with Wolof words was published in *The Times* for July 19th, 1969. Herskovits discusses and dismisses the 'thousand-mile theory' in *Myth*, pp. 35–6, and Captain Samuel Gamble is quoted in *A History of Sierra Leone 1400–1787*, by Peter Kup, Cambridge University Press, 1961, p. 90.

In his *Travels* (above) Mungo Park describes the instruments of the Mandingoes and the '*jilli kea*' on p. 213, and the journey with the slow slave coffle on pp. 248–77. The story of Abu Bakr is told in *Africa Remembered – Narratives by West Africans from the Era of the Slave*, ed. Philip D. Curtin (University of Wisconsin, 1967), where extracts from Olaudah Equiano also appear. For Abu Bakr, see pp. 161–2. In *Slave Songs* Lydia Parrish quotes Sir Charles Lyell on African Tom on p. 24, and on p. 26 discusses Sālih Bilālī whose *Recollections of Massina* appear in *Africa Remembered*. The quotation comes from p. 151. Ulrich B. Phillips' *American Negro Slavery; a Survey of the Supply, Employment and Control of Negro Labour as determined by the Plantation Regime* was published by D. Appleton and Company in 1918, while Elizabeth Donnan's *Documents Illustrative of the Slave Trade to America* (Carnegie Institution, 1930–5) remains an indispensable source-work. The quotation from Roland Oliver and R. D. Fage comes from pp. 120–1 of their *A Short History of Africa* (Penguin Books, 1962), and that from Church, Clarke, Clarke and Henderson's *Africa and the Islands* (as above) is on p. 67. Note that the apparently conflicting figures for the slave trade as given by these authors refers to the *total* of slaves exported to *all* the Americas.

The reminiscences of New Orleans by Benjamin Henry Latrobe are quoted by Kmen in *Music in New Orleans*, pp. 227–8 and Stearns in *The Story of Jazz*, p. 51. Herbert Asbury's *The French Quarter* (Alfred A. Knopf), pp. 240–4, gives full descriptions of the reports of Congo Square. Cable's *The Dance in Place Congo* has been noted above – the descriptions of slaves come from pp. 372–80 in *Creoles and Cajuns*. Note, incidentally, that the Foulah were probably *not* mis-called 'poulards' – the tribe is known as Peul in the previous French colonies. Niles Newbell Puckett in *Folk Beliefs of the Southern Negro* (Chapel Hill, 1926), notes other African words in addition to *gris-gris* on p. 16. The description of Jean Montanet by Lafcadio Hearn comes from the article 'The Last of the Voudoos' in *Harpers Weekly*, for November 7th, 1885, and the supression of drums is noted by Herskovits in *Myth* on p. 138. Finally, the concluding quotation from James A. Porter comes from his article on 'The Trans-Cultural Affinities of African Art' which appeared in Waterman's 'Influence' in Sol Tax's *Acculturation in the Americas*, p. 125.

Chapter 5. Africa and the Blues
Gus Cannon's description of his first banjo is quoted from a recorded interview on the album *American Skiffle Bands* (Folkways FA2610), Big Bill Broonzy's guitar is described on p. 8 of *Big Bill Blues* (Cassell, 1955) and the note on Big Joe Williams' instrument was published in Dave Mangurian's article on him in *Jazz Journal* for December 1963. Dave Evans published his article on 'Reverend Rubin Lacy' in *Blues Unlimited* for January 1967 and Mack McCormick's notes on Mance Lipscomb accompany the album *Mance Lipscomb, Texas Sharecropper and Songster* (Arhoolie F1001). The quotation from Hobart Smith comes from an article 'I Just got the Music in my Head' in *Sing Out!* for January 1964, and from Dock Boggs in an article

'I Always Loved the Lonésome Songs' in *Sing Out !* for July 1964. Tony Russell's study *Blacks, Whites and Blues* (Studio Vista 1970), studies the Negro-white interchange of song and blues traditions in detail.

The 'Small Farmer's' who described music on their plantations are quoted in full in *The Negro and His Folk-Lore* (see above) pp. 345–6 and 350–1, and the quotation from the slave Cato appears in *Lay My Burden Down*, ed. B. A. Botkin (University of Chicago Press, 1945), p. 86.

On the possible use of anthropological techniques of analysis the article on 'Anthropological Implications of Sickle Cell Gene Distribution in West Africa', by Frank B. Livingstone, which was published in *American Anthropologist*, vol. 60, no. 3, 1958, pp. 533–62, was of great interest. Derek F. Roberts' study of 'The Dynamics of Racial Intermixture in the American Negro – Some Anthropological Considerations' was published in the *American Journal of Human Genetics*, vol 7, no. 4, pp. 361–7, in answer to a previous study on 'The Dynamics of Racial Intermixture – An Analysis based on the American Negro' by Bentley Glass and C. C. Li published in the same journal for volume 5, no. 1, 1953. Herskovits' *The American Negro – A Study In Racial Crossing* (1928) has been reprinted by the Indiana University Press, 1964, while similarly C. G. Seligman's *Races of Africa* (1930) has been reprinted by the Oxford University Press, 1966, the quotation coming from pp. 35–7. Dr Bentley Glass published the paper 'On the Unlikelihood of Significant Admixture of Genes from the North American Indians in the Present Composition of the Negroes of the United States' in the *American Journal for Human Genetics* in the same issue as Derek F. Roberts' paper above, pp. 368–85.

Lorenzo Turner's linguistic studies have already been noted; mention should also be made of his paper 'African Survivals in the New World with Special Emphasis on the Arts' in *Africa From the Point of View of American Scholars* (Présence Africaine, 1958), pp. 101–6. Dr David Dalby's article in *The Times* for July 19, 1969, from whence these examples come, has also been noted above. The comments on blue notes by Charles Duvelle appear in his notes to *Haute Volta* (Disques Ocora SOR10) and John Fahey's 'Textual and Musicological Analysis of the Recordings of Charley Patton' was a Master's Thesis for the Department of Mythology and Folklore at University College of Los Angeles, 1965. The list of categories of Hausa music was published by David Ames in the notes to *Nigeria-Hausa Music 11* (UNESCO BM30L2307). In his *Urban Blues* (University of Chicago Press, 1966), Charles Keil shows 'Big Bobby Blue Bland on Stage' in Chapter V and discusses 'Role and Response' in Chapter VI.

ACKNOWLEDGMENTS

I am grateful to a number of people for their help in drawing my attention to books, other publications and recordings while I was engaged in collecting material for this study; my thanks to them all.

My special thanks, however, must go to Professor J. H. Kwabena Nketia for inviting me to lecture at the Institute of African Studies, University of Ghana, and for giving me every facility to record tribal music while there. Sincere thanks, too, to John Lloyd, then Dean of the Faculty of Architecture at Kumasi University of Science and Technology for bringing me to Ghana, and for accompanying myself and my wife on the field trip to Nangodi, and for much advice and help with recording. Dr Colin Painter, who was lecturing in linguistics in 1964 at the University of Ghana and who is now in the Department of Linguistics at the University of Indianapolis, has continually advised and opened up new lines of enquiry for which I am very grateful. I am particularly indebted to M. Charles Duvelle, General Editor of the Collection Radiodiffusion Outre-Mer (Disques Ocora) for help in many ways, including the loan of photographs and access to recordings; and to Folkways Scholastic Records for much help with recorded material – my warm appreciation to them both; also to Colin Fournier, whose help with translations was most valuable. Finally I must express my sincere appreciation to my partner in the study of the Texas Blues, Mack McCormick, whose insistence that the problem of African retentions in the blues be re-examined caused this introductory study to be written.

PAUL OLIVER

RECORD LIST

Comparative Recordings

NEGRO FOLK MUSIC OF AFRICA AND AMERICA
Edited by Harold Courlander   Ethnic Folkways FE4500 (two records)
Twenty-four examples from Africa and the Americas. West Africa represented by Ibo and Yoruba recordings only. United States – examples of unaccompanied songs only. Items of interest include a Juba dance from Haiti and Shango cult song from Trinidad recorded by Herskovits.

AFRICAN AND AFRO-AMERICAN DRUMS
Edited by Harold Courlander   Ethnic Folkways FE4502 (two records)
Similar collection with West African examples from the Yoruba only. North American items confined to jazz drumming by Baby Dodds, and a remarkable children's street band recorded in New York.

African Collections

AFRIQUE NOIRE: Panorama de la Musique Instrumentale   Bam (France) LD409A
A broad selection edited by Charles Duvelle of Ocora recordings, including Lobi and Malinke xylophones, lute and bowed monochords from Niger and drum orchestras in Dahomey.

SOUNDS OF AFRICA, edited by Andrew Tracey   Verve Forecast (A) FVS9510
Stereo collection of fragmentary recordings. Unequal, but includes Mali lutes, Senegal *kora*.

MUSIC FROM WEST AFRICA, recorded by Gilbert Rouget   Vogue (F) LVLX193
Recordings of Baoulé in Ivory Coast with drum orchestras, flutes, xylophone, contrasted with Malinké recordings from Guinea including outstanding xylophone orchestras, *kora*, water-drum, harp and harp-lute. Valuable contrast of forest and Savannah cultures.

PONDO KAKOU, recorded by Gilbert Rouget   Vogue (F) MC20.141
Baoulé ritual contrasted with Yoruba drums from Dahomey and recordings of harps and harp-lutes of the Malinké in Guinea.

West African Rain Forest Peoples

DRUMS OF THE YORUBA OF NIGERIA   Ethnic Folkways (A) FE4441
Recorded by William Bascom, examples of Igbin drums, Dundun drums and Bàtá drums. Also recordings of Sàngó cult drumming.

MUSIQUES DAHOMÉENNES, recorded by Charles Duvelle   Ocora OCR17
Drum orchestras accompanying dances, and ritual drumming. Also popular orchestra with drums, *sansa* and monochord. Side-blown flutes and musical bow.

MUSIQUE KABRÉ (North Togoland)   Ocora (F) OCR16
Instrumentally primitive bamboo flutes and log xylophone, but including remarkable 'lithophone' rhyhms on basalt stones. Recorded by Raymond Verdier.

THE BAOULÉ OF THE IVORY COAST, recorded by Donald Thurow
       Ethnic Folkways FE4476

MUSIQUE BAOULÉ KODÈ, recorded by Charles Duvelle   Ocora (F) OCR34
Mainly drum orchestras with both featuring Goli festival and extended 'Congassa' ritual of Baoulé Kodè. Former record has horns, flute and rare Baoulé harp.

THE MUSIC OF THE DAN, recorded by Hugo Zemp   Baren Reiter (UNESCO) BM30L2301
Drums for various rites and accompanying work. Also mirlitons, and hunter's harp borrowed from Malinké. Includes Malinké musicians from north.

FOLK MUSIC OF LIBERIA, recorded by Packard Okie   Ethnic Folkways (A) FE4465
Various tribes and descendants of repatriated slaves. Recordings of work songs, slit drums, belly harp and Mandingo balafon played by Mandingo settlers from north.

West African Savannah Peoples

DANSES ET CHANTS BAMOUN, recorded by Michel Houdry   Ocora (F) SOR3
Sansa, Cameroon lyre *mvet*, drums and horns for Sultans of Bamoun.

ANTHOLOGIE DE LA MUSIQUE DU TCHAD
Recorded by Charles Duvelle and Michel Vuylstèke   Ocora (F) OCR36/37/38 (three records)
Extensive survey of music of the Sara, the peoples of west Mayo-Kebbi and professional Islamic musicians. Drums, xylophones, horns, lutes, arc-harps, *algaita* and long trumpets of considerable diversity of styles.

NIGERIA – HAUSA MUSIC, Volumes One and Two
Recorded by David Wason Ames   Baren Reiter (UNESCO) BM30L2306 and BM30L2307
Twenty-four items showing wide range of Hausa music illustrating Ames' classification of functions of music in this society. Drums, lutes, fiddles, orchestras for *bori* cult, for accompanying trades and work. Music of professional entertainers.

NIGER – LA MUSIQUE DES GRIOTS   Ocora (F) OCR20
Recorded by Tolia Nikiprowetzky; gives excellent picture of the music of *griots*, solo, duet and in orchestras, including *goge*, *godjié*, *garaya*.

NOMADES DU NIGER (Tuareg and Bororo), recorded by Tolia Nikiprowetzky
Ocora (F) OCR29

TUAREG MUSIC OF THE SOUTHERN SAHARA
Recorded by Finola and Geoffrey Holiday   Ethnic Folkways FE4470
The former includes virtuoso performances on the *inzad* one-string fiddle. Also water drums and
flute. The Folkways issue mainly features songs with water drum and a striking Tazenkharet
dance shared with Arabs and Negro Africans.

MUSIC OF MALI, recorded by Betty and W. Gurnee Dyer   Ethnic Folkways FE4338

LES DOGON, recorded by François Di Dio   Ocora (F) OCR33
Both records emphasise the drum music of the Dogon on calabash drums. The former also has
recordings from Timbuktu and Tuareg lute players.

HAUTE VOLTA, recorded by Charles Duvelle   Ocora (F) SOR10
A striking collection of Bambara xylophone, *kondé* lute, musical bow, *sansa*, calabash drum
orchestra from various parts of Upper Volta.

WOLOF MUSIC OF SENEGAL AND THE GAMBIA, recorded by David Ames
Ethnic Folkways FE4462
Professional entertainers and story tellers (*gewel*), accompanied by *halam*. Also drum rhythms
for dances among the Wolof.

THE MUSIC OF THE DIOLA-FOGNY OF THE CASAMANCE, SENEGAL
Recorded by J. David Sapir   Ethnic Folkways (A) FE4323
Important recordings of Diola work-songs with extensive notes and translations. Also extempore
song, and fetish dances.

LA MUSIQUE DES GRIOTS – SENEGAL, recorded by Tolia Nikiprowetzky
Ocora (F) OCR15
Outstanding collection of the music of the *griots* with exceptional examples of *kora*, monochords,
solo, duet and group performances, from tribes represented in Senegal.

ACCOMPANYING RECORD

Blind Darby: *Meat And Bread Blues*. Ladzekpo and Ewe Drum
Orchestra: *Agbekor*. Mamprusi Tribesmen: *Ring Dance*. The
Como Drum Band: *Oh Baby*. Orchestra of Bour Fodé Diouf:
Wong. George 'Bongo Joe' Coleman: *Eloise*. Hassan Danlado
griots: Bako. Elder Richard Bryant's Sanctified Singers: *Lord, Lord
He Sure Is Good To Me*. Kunaal and Sosira: *Praise Song*. Butch
Cage and Willie Thomas: *Forty-Four Blues*. Lanyare and Lobi
Tribesmen: *Sabere*. Thiam Sy *griots: Halam Improvisation*.
Lonnie Colman: *Wild About My Loving*. Walter Roland: *Jookit
Jookit*. Maïkaï: *Babaï*. Robert Johnson: *Stop Breakin' Down
Blues*.

GLOSSARY OF INSTRUMENTS

Apart from the instruments mentioned in the text which are indexed here (those page numbers in italic being to illustrations or to reference-only in illustration captions), a number of instruments used by West African peoples have been added to this glossary, which, however, is representative only and in no way complete. Most of the West African instruments listed may be heard on recordings issued in Europe and the United States. The names of the instruments vary from tribe to tribe and their spelling has not been standardised.

Abeng, collective term for horn instruments among Akan peoples

Abitin, Timne term for drum, Sierra Leone

Adabatram, Ewe war drum, Ghana and Togoland

Adedemma, Akan vertical pegged drum with wedged feet

Adewu, Ewe drum for hunting ceremonial, Ghana

Agonga, cylindrical drum of the Tuareg, Mali and Niger

Akalumbe, harp of the Timne, Sierra Leone

Akonde, Susu fiddle, Sierra Leone

Akoroma, drum of Ashanti warrior societies

Akrima, egg-cup shaped drum, hand beaten, Dahomey

Akukuadwo, semi-cylindrical, slightly tapered Ashanti drum

Algaïta, shawm of the Hausa and Tuareg, but widely used in Savannah regions 52, 71

Anuman, whistle of the Baule, Ivory Coast

Apentemma, large bottle-shaped Ashanti drum used in Akan orchestras 30

Asiko, frame drum of the Yoruba, Western Nigeria and Dahomey

Asokoben, Ashanti elephant tusk horn

Assakhalabo, water drum made from floating calabash, Tuareg

Atsimevu, five-foot-long master drum of Ewe drum orchestras, Ghana and Togo 35, 36

Atukpani, pair of drums, male and female, of Ewe drum orchestra

Atumpan, pair of drums, male and female; principal talking drums of Ashanti 29, 30

Bala, correct term for West African xylophone in Guinea, Senegal, Mali: see Balafon

Balafon (also **Balafou, balafeu**), European term for the **bala**. Fo or fon means literally, 'to speak'. 53, 55, 56, 71, 72, 96

Bania, Senegal lute with three or four strings, which probably gave its name to the banjo 50, 55

Banjar (also **banger**), early name for the banjo in North America 50

Banjo, plucked chordophone of West African origin, developed in North America, originally with four strings, the fifth being added in the early nineteenth century 19, 20, 21, 23, 25, 39, 50, 56, 78, 84, 86, 87, 88, 95

Baradundu, calabash drum of the Dyoula

Baratyu, Mandingo calabash drum similar to the Baradundu

Bàtá, drum family used for the worship of Sàngó. Yoruba, Western Nigeria; also conical drum with laced heads of the Yoruba. 32

Batá, drum of the Nago of Dahomey

Batta, spherical calabash drum of the Hausa, Northern Nigeria

Belly harp, European term for West African harp with half-gourd resonator held against the stomach 42, 45

Bennde, large drum of the Dyoula

Beta, musical bow of the Ewe, Togo

Bolange, Susu xylophone with twenty wooden bars on frame structure

Bolo, three-stringed harp-lute of the Fulah, Sierra Leone

Bolon, three-stringed harp of the Malinké and Senufo, Mali and Ivory Coast

Bondofo, Mandingo side-blown antelope horn

Bones, animal bones, shaped and carved to present flat surfaces which clack when vibrated between the fingers, North America 22

Boumpa, length of cane, slit and side-blown, with calabash resonators at each end, Upper Volta

B'ru, trumpet of the Dyoula

Bulu, side-blown horn, Mende, Sierra Leone

Bulumbata, large arched harp of Senegambia, with gourd resonator, ten strings, and metal vibrator 48

Buru, Mandingo side-blown horn, made of wood or ivory

Buru, Bambara horn, Upper Volta

Dawuro, Ashanti slit gong or conical gong 30

Dale, Lobi drum made from neck of a broken pot 52, 55

Donno, hour-glass tension drum of the Ashanti, Ghana 29, 30

Dundu, widespread term for a drum among Mandingo- and Mende-speaking peoples

Dundufa, two-headed drum played to stimulate trade for butchers among Hausa

Dundun, large hour-glass tension drum, Yoruba of Western Nigeria and Dahomey 32

Dyegele, Senufo xylophone with twelve bars on wood frame

Earth bow, presumed origin of the North American washtub bass, made from hide membrane stretched over depression in the ground. String attached to one side of the depression, and to a length of wood. Generally found in Congo and Central Africa. 36

Ekpe, friction drum of Efik in South-East Nigeria

Elong, xylophone of fourteen bars, Lobi of Upper Volta: cf. **gil**

Etwie, friction drum of the Baoule, used to imitate a leopard

Farai, medium-length horn, Northern Nigeria 52

Furi, three-hole end-blown flute, Niger

Garaya, two-stringed lute, over five feet long including resonator, Niger *51*
Gah-gah, percussion gourd widely used by Savannah *griots*
Ganga, Hausa drum. Generic term for drum in Upper Volta, Niger, Northern Nigeria. *52*
Gangana, Dogon percussion bell
Gangano, drum of the Mossi, Upper Volta
Gangalan, Tuareg cylindrical drum
Gankogui, clapperless bell of the Ewe, Ghana
Gil, xylophone of the Ghana and Ivory Coast Lobi *53, 53–5*
Gimbeh, bottle-shaped drum with metal vibrators attached, Fulah, Sierra Leone
Gingiru, Dogon harp-lute, Mali
Gnaghour, bowed monochord *96*
Goge, gogué, calabash fiddle with single string of hair, played with arched bow, widely used among Savannah peoples *51, 87*
Gogeru, Fulbe fiddle with two or three strings, Cameroun
Goly, Baoule monochord, Ivory Coast
Gong-gong, European/pidgin term for the Ashanti clapperless bell or gong
Gorong, Wolof upright log drum, Senegal and Gambia
Gouroumi, three-string lute, over a metre in length, Niger *51, 96*
Gudu-gudu, Yoruba kettledrum, Western Nigeria and Dahomey
Gui dounou, Malinké water drum of similar kind to the Tuareg type. Guinea

Halam, five-stringed lute of the Wolof and other Senegambian tribes, with three open strings *49, 50, 96*
Harp lute, chordophone indigenous to West Africa with the strings in a plane rising vertically from the belly of the instrument

Igbin, drum-family for the worship of Obàtálá, Yoruba *32*
Inzad, Imzhad, Tuareg bowed monochord, generally played by the women *62*
Ikoro, Ibo ritual long drum, Nigerian Eastern region
Isanzi, West African sansa, or 'thumb piano'
Iyá Ilù, Yoruba tension drum in Dundun and Bàtá orchestras

Jawbone, jawbone of a mule, ass, cow or other domestic animal used as a rattle. A North American plantation instrument. The jawbone was also struck or played with a nail or length of iron.
Jojo, drum of the Fulbe, Senegal

Kakaki, long trumpet of Nigerian emirates, six feet or more in length *52*
Kalangual, Fulbe hour-glass drum, Cameroun
Kalungu, Hausa hour-glass drum, Nigeria
Kambreh, plectrum lute played widely in the Savannah regions – Niger, Sierra Leone, and Senegal
Kanango, Yoruba hour-glass tension drum
Kani, triangular frame zither with seven strings, Kru, Sierra Leone
Karaning, Mandingo monochord spike fiddle
Kasso, harp lute of the Gambia with twenty-two strings, cf. **Seron**, kora
Kazoo, submarine-shaped tube mirliton, played in blues bands *38*
Kele, drum of the Nago, Dahomey
Kele, side-blown flute of the Dogon, Mali
Kele, Mende slit-drum with three slits along its length, Sierra Leone
Kete, four-hole notched flute, Ghana: also Ashanti drum orchestra for chiefs
Khalam, alternative spelling for the Wolof **halam** lute

Kidi, Ewe vertical barrel drum, Ghana and Togoland *34*
Ko, hunter's harp of the Dan, Ivory Coast, with six strings in two parallel rows *49*
Komo, two-stringed lute with long bowl of calabash and with metal vibrator, Nigeria, Hausa
Kone, sansa of Upper Volta
Koni, six-stringed harp-lute played for hunting by the Malinke and borrowed by the Senufo, Guinea and Ivory Coast *49*
Koonting, three-stringed Mandingo lute, as noted by Mungo Park *71*
Kontigui, plucked monochord of the Songhai, Niger
Kor, stem-based drum, Lobi *54*
Kora, massive twenty-one stringed harp-lute of the Senegal *griots* *46, 47, 48, 72*
Kori, six-stringed harp-lute of the Senufo, Ivory Coast
Korro, Mungo Park's term for the **kora** *71, 72*
Kukuma, horsehair-strung monochord bowed fiddle, Hausa, Nigeria *51, 87*
Kundye, Soso monochord bowed fiddle, Guinea
Kunting, three-stringed Mandingo lute
Kusukurum, master drum used in *apirede* orchestras of Ashanti paramount chiefs, Ghana
Kyirem, drum orchestra for Ashanti warrior associations

Lamba, large drum of the Wolof, Senegambia
Lontoré, flute of Upper Volta tribes
Lunga, large drum of the Mossi, Upper Volta
Lunga, Dyoula hour-glass drum

Marimba, African xylophone with slats of wood on a frame, each slat having a gourd resonator. The Marimba was brought to Central and South America. *55, 78*
Marimba brett, African **sansa** as noted by Cable in New Orleans *78*
Musical bow, hunting bow used as a musical instrument, or musical arc patterned on the hunting bow, tapped or plucked, with sometimes a gourd resonator, or with the mouth used as a resonator. In the latter instance known as a *mouth bow*. Widely found in hunting cultures not only in Africa. *42*
Mvet, four-string lyre with calabash resonator, Cameroun

Ngenge, Fula monochord spike fiddle with movable bridge, Sierra Leone
Ngùne, Mandingo monochord fiddle, Guinea
Nsambi, home-made fiddle, of European influence, Congo *26*
Ntumpan, alternative spelling for **Atumpan**

Odurugya, Ashanti end-blown cane flute, Ghana
Ogidàn drums, drum orchestra used for the worship of *Ogun*, Yoruba, Nigeria *32*

Pampane, long wooden trumpet, Fulbe
Papo, side-blown split reed wind instrument with calabash resonators, Dahomey
Para, arched harp, Niger
Petia, drum used in Ashanti *adowa* bands for social dancing *30*
Pira, iron castanets to accompany Lobi orchestras, Ghana and Ivory Coast *52, 54*
Pomsa, two-string lute, Niger

Ramkie, remkie, three- or four-stringed guitar related to the Portuguese *rabequinha* brought from Malabar to South Africa and developed by the Cape Hottentots. Also *rábekin, ramakienjo, raamakie, ramki*. *26, 27*
Rasp, notched wood, gourd or metal instru-

ment against which a rod is moved rhythmically. The **washboard** may be a North American equivalent.

Rattle, African rattles are frequently made of gourds with beans inside or strung on the outside of the instrument. Other rattles may be woven of basketwork.

Raft zither, **raft harp**, zither made of several lengths of cane bound together in a raft-like form. Each cane has a split length which forms the 'string', the lengths being raised over cane bridges. *79*

Riti, Gambian monochord spike fiddle

Riti, four-string spike fiddle, Guinea *45*

Sabar, long Wolof hour-glass drum

Sangu, Ewe **sansa**

Sanku, harp-lute with two rows of strings, Guinea

Sansa, **sanza**, African 'thumb piano', or linguaphone, with a number of metal or cane tongues raised over a bridge. Sansas may be built over gourds or small containers and are played with thumbs or with fingers of both hands. *78, 79, 84, 96*

Seke, calabash rattle, Ghana

Sérendou, side-blown flute played by herders in Upper Volta

Seron, Malinke variant of the **kora** with fifteen to twenty strings *48*

Shekere, gourd rattle of the Yoruba

Simbing, seven-stringed lute-harp, Mandingo

Slit drums, log or bamboo drums with longitudinal slits opening to a hollowed interior

Sogo, Ewe barrel-shaped drum, Ghana *34*

Soku, Mandingo bowed chordophone

Stickado, Ibo instrument probably in xylophone form, though a slapstick has also been suggested

Tabala, large sacred drum of the Wolof. Also a Mandingo warning drum. *71*

Tabl, generic term for drum in Arab countries

Tamande, Mandingo drum, generic term: also **tamba**

Tangtang, Mandingo drum with one end open *71*

Tamatama, Tuareg term for drum

Tama, Senegalese tension drum, held under armpit

Tension drum, drum of hour-glass shape with skin membranes at both ends. These are tightened by thongs which extend between both heads and are compressed by the elbow or upper arm.

Tinde, Tuareg drum played by the women. It consists of a length of hide hand-held in tension over a mortar or gourd vessel.

Tomba, Mandingo hour-glass drum

Washboard, washwoman's rubbing board, used as a rhythm instrument by rubbing its surface with spoons, nails, or with the fingers clad in thimbles. Rhythm instrument in blues bands in the United States. *38*

Washtub bass, inverted washtub with string attached to one side and affixed to the end of a broom-handle held against the rim. When tautened it can be used as a one-string bass. May be derived from the **earth bow** (q.v.). *36, 38, 39*

Water drum, **water gourd**, an upturned calabash floating in a larger vessel half filled with water. The inner calabash is played with sticks.

West African harp, indigenous harp made from a number of separately strung arcs joined at a common stem or resonator *42*

Xylophone, Melanesian in origin and brought via Madagascar to Africa. The African xylophone in its simplest form consists of a number of logs placed across the legs of the player. More advanced xylophones are fixed to a frame or slung over a trough frame. Under the slats of the latter, gourds are placed as resonators. *41, 42, 53, 55, 78*

Zanze, alternative spelling for **sansa**

Further details on musical instruments of West Africa may be found in the books and other references cited in the notes to chapters: in the liner notes to issued recordings: in 'Terms for Musical Instruments in the Sudanic Languages', by Helen E. Hause, in *Supplement to the Journal of the American Oriental Society*, volume 68, 1948: and in *Musical Instruments, A Comprehensive Dictionary*, which has a detailed bibliography, by Sibyl Marcuse, published by Doubleday & Co., U.S.A., 1964, and *Country Life*, U.K., 1966.

INDEX OF TRIBES AND PEOPLE

Tribes and peoples of Africa mentioned in the text are listed. Their location in relation to national political boundaries is given, but such boundaries have little relation to the distribution of tribes. For the territorial areas where the peoples are centred see the map on page 69. The spelling of African tribal names is not standardised but English and French alternatives are given where relevant. Page numbers in *italic* indicate illustrations.

Akan. Peoples of Ashanti and related regions, Ghana and Ivory Coast   6, 32, 34

Ashanti. Dominant people of a federation of tribes in the old Gold Coast (Ghana)   7, 9, 17, 29, *30*, 32, 39, 42, 52, 54, 55, 61, 68, 69, 73, *74*, *75*, 81, *82*, 87, 90, 91

Bambara. Extensive savannah people in south-west Mali   39, 55, 56, 61, 72, 73, 75, 76, 79, 80, 81, 82, 88, 91, 93

Baule, Baoule. Kwa-speaking people, one of the Akan tribes, of Ivory Coast   39, 61, 82, 87

Beriberi, Béri-béri. Kanurac people situated north of the Hausa in Bornu province   52, 75

Bobo. Primitive tribe of Upper Volta   39, 82, 93

Busanni, Boussani. Tribe of Nigritic stock, Upper Volta   65, 66

Dahomeans (Fon). Correctly termed Fon, but frequently identified with Dahomey, where they live   17, 61, 68, 69, 74

Dan. Tribe in Ivory Coast to north-west of region close to Guinea Malinke   48, 49, 82

Dioula, Dyoula. Scattered people of Soninke stock, mainly in Upper Volta. Not related to Diola, Diola-Fogny (q.v.)

Diola, Diola-Fogny. Small coastal tribe of the Basse Casamance of Senegal   41, 57, 58, 61, 75

Dogon. Cliff-dwelling people of Mali   39, 61, 82

Efik. Bantoid-speaking people of southern Nigeria   68, 75

Ekoi. South-west Nigerian people of Cross River region   91

Ewe. Twi-speaking people of Togoland and eastern Ghana, related to Fon of Dahomey   32, *33*, *34*, 39, 42, 68, 87, 90

Fanti. Small coastal tribe, Ghana   73, 90

Fon. Dahomey people related to Ewe - *see* **Dahomeans**

Fra-Fra. Sub-tribe of Grusi complex, Northern Ghana   4, 5, *101*

Fula, Fulah, Fulani, Fulbe, Peul. Nomadic, or semi-nomadic, pastoral people, widely scattered across West Africa. Other spellings include the early Feloop. Some Fulani are relatively settled, notably those of the Fouta Toro region of Senegal   41, 49, 61, 68, 69, 70, 73, 74, 75, 76, 79, 90

Ga. Small coastal tribe in Ghana in whose territory stood a number of slave castles   6, 35

Ghimira, Gidole. Peoples of Ethiopia   58

Grusi, Grunshi. Complex of small tribes in border region of Ghana and Upper Volta (see also, Fra-Fra)   5

Guere, Guere-Wobe, Ngere. Tribe related to the Dan, Ivory Coast   49, 82

111

Hausa, Haoussa. Extensive Muslim people in northern Nigeria, and Niger   7, 50, 51, 52, 58, 59, 61, 63, 68, 69, 75, 77, 88, 98

Ibo. Large tribe of Eastern region of Nigeria (Biafra)   31, 32, 39, 68, 75, 82, 90
Ila. Tribe in the Middle Zambesi region   24

Jolof, Jaloff. *See* **Wolof**

Kagoro. Scattered people part Bambara, Soninke and Fulani   89
Kru. Coastal tribal complex, Liberia   41

Lobi. People inhabiting region at intersection of Upper Volta, Ivory Coast and Ghana   51, 53, 54, 55

Mande, Manding, Mandingo. Mande-speaking peoples of which the Malinke are the largest. Many references to 'Mandingo' are really to Malinke, but also applied loosely to Bambara, Soninke and others   39, 41, 48, 55, 58, 68, 69, 70, 72, 76, 78, 80, 88, 90, 91, 92
Mandingo. *See* **Mande**
Malinke. Extensively distributed tribe occupying large areas of Senegal, Guinea and western Ivory Coast   39, 48, 49, 55, 61
Mende. Sierra Leone tribe situated near the coast   68, 69
Mina. Small tribe related to Ewe, Ghana and Togo   68
Mossi. Widely distributed people of Mali and Upper Volta   39, 68, 82

Nupe. Southern Nigerian complex of tribes   68
Nzima. Small coastal tribe, Ghana   6

Peul. *See* **Fulani**
Pygmies. Diminutive forest-dwelling people of the Congo   58

Senufo. Extensively distributed people of the Ivory Coast   49
Songhai. Ancient people of northern savannah region of Niger and Mali and of distinct linguistic stock   92
Soninke. Moslem people related to Malinke, inhabiting north-western Mali and northern Senegal   39, 91
Susu. Moslem coastal tribe, Guinea   61

Temne. Coastal tribe, Sierra Leone   68, 70
Toma. Tribe related to the Dan, Sierra Leone and Liberia interior   60
Tonga. People of the Middle Zambesi   26
Tuareg. Nomadic people of Berber stock but independent culture, extensively distributed, including Niger, Mali   61, 62
Twi. Complex of tribes speaking Twi languages. *See* **Ashanti, Ewe**

Vai. Small coastal tribe, Sierra Leone, Ivory Coast and Liberia   70, 91

Wolof, Joloff, Jalof. Large indigenous tribe in the Senegambia   41, 46, 49, 50, 61, 68, 70, 75, 76, 88, 93
Wyda, Whydah. Coastal tribe of Dahomey engaged in the slave trade   75

Yoruba. Widely distributed people of western Nigeria and Dahomey   17, 32, 39, 42, 52, 61, 68, 69, 74, 75, 81, 87, 90, 91

DATE DUE

APR 23 1979

GAYLORD

PRINTED IN U.S.A